# Over the Hills & Far Away

# Over the Hills

# &

# Far Away

---

## by Rob Collister

THE ERNEST PRESS

Published by The Ernest Press 1996
© Copyright Rob Collister

'

British Library Cataloguing-in-Publication Data
A Catalogue record for this book is available
from the British Library

ISBN 0 948153 40 7

Maps drawn by Jeremy Ashcroft

Typeset by Askvik Språktjenester A/S, Norway
Printed by St. Edmundsbury Press

# Acknowledgements

My grateful thanks to:

Helen Berry for speedy and accurate word processing and helpful suggestions;

Netti, my wife, for proof-reading, constructive comment and infinite forbearance;

Jim Perrin and Ken Wilson for advice and encouragement;

and, last but not least, Peter Hodgkiss and Jack Baines for their commitment to mountaineering literature.

Most of the articles published here have appeared before in magazines, journals and anthologies. For permission to re-use the material, my thanks to the editors of the Alpine Journal, Climber, and The Great Outdoors; and to Peter Cliff, Baton Wicks and Mitchell-Beazley.

# TABLE OF CONTENTS

## The Quality of the Experience

## Wilderness Ways

# Home Ground

# GOING TO WORK (1984)

Quietly, at dawn, I leave the small stone house at the head of the cwm and pass, shrinking, through dew-drop dripping rushes which drench my trousers instantly. A reluctant jog takes me up a field where, later in the year, mountain pansies bloom briefly before the sheep find them, to the edge of the forest. A ride of rank grass runs straight as a conifer trunk up the steep spruce-smothered hillside. I grind up it in low gear, head down with effort, noticing the pointed droppings with which a fox has waymarked his route. He had our chickens last autumn. In a soggy patch at the top of the ride grows that lovely golden flower, bog asphodel. But this is April and there are no flowers in the mountains yet, save in a few favoured nooks and crannies, the purple saxifrage. Up here, the dew has sharpened to frost which scrunches crisply beneath my studded shoes until I emerge, panting, into sunlight on the crest of the ridge. The hardest part of the journey over, I pause to gaze around, glad now to be up so early, grateful to be alive. Below, the forest is draped darkly, threateningly, around the few surviving fields and their vein-like tracery of stone-walls. Further down the valley, the trees have disappeared; in their place the splintered wreckage of a felled hillside. The value of landscape, however real, is intangible and beyond the comprehension of economists, even in a National Park. I raise my eyes to familiar mountain shapes, Arenig, Manod, Moelwyn, white and glistening, holding spring at arm's length, and feel better.

The far side of the ridge is a richly glowing carpet of gold and emerald, the drab, drooping fronds of dead bracken and the workaday mossy masses of polytrichum transformed by the early morning sun. Descent is a delight, a series of flying leaps over this soft, forgiving surface down to a stony track. A village comes in sight, straggling along a valley bottom. It is the grey of slate, accepting its place in the landscape, only the occasional white-washed cottage standing out aggressively, like a stranger. Not far away, deserted quarries are disappearing beneath trees. Prominent on a knoll, stands a gaunt stone tower, relic of a troubled past. A heron lifts heavily from the riverbank and flaps gravely away.

Smoke rises straight into the cold, still air from every chimney-pot, but there is not a soul to be seen as I run through the village. Soon, I am climbing a wet, narrow lane bright with celandine and violet and golden saxifrage, into another conifer forest. Among the younger trees I have often seen black grouse and heard the fishing-reel note of a grasshopper-warbler. But the trees are growing fast and today I see only the odd wren scuttling among stacked logs and chaffinches bustling about in pairs. Without regret, I surface from the forest onto open moorland where a stone-chat greets me cheerfully from a spray of gorse. The snow-streaked rocks of Siabod rise on my left, ahead lie the rolling white tops of the Carneddau, dappled capriciously with sunlight. My stride lengthens, as much in response to this scene as to an easing of the angle. The grassy track passes within feet of two hut circles, barely distinguishable now. Two heaps of stones nearby are cairns enclosing stone coffins built long ago, in warmer, drier times, when men lived up here. My mind jerks back to the present as I notice cattle across the path. The broad brow and massive shoulders of the bull stand out long before I see the ring in his nose, and I give him a wide berth. Bulls, even placid Welsh Blacks, are no respecters of rights of way.

The track twists stonily downwards through oak woodland of a type that must have covered most of Wales once, into a new valley. Only another mile to go now, at first on a surfaced road, then along the banks of a rocky little river disturbing dippers and grey wagtails and ewes with tiny wobbly-legged lambs. Finally, a forest track brings me to the edge of a lake which mirrors the perfection of the morning and I cross a footbridge, famous for its view of the Horseshoe, to my destination.

A shower and a change of clothes and I am ready for work

# FIRE (1974)

I lie on one elbow before a fire
Of ash and elm. The trees were downed last month
In the gales, the logs split an hour ago —
The devil to split, that elm!
Body warm one flank wood warm the other,
Content, the dog lies close beside me.
Outside, fresh gusts tear at brown-leaved oaks
Scouring a sky emptied by the moon
Baring a big night full of frost, and noise.

Over the fireplace are chrysanthemums
And various objects, the gifts of friends:
Carefully-blown, an emperor penguin's egg;
Squatting on its haunches, enigmatic,
A hollow creature from America —
Frog, or cat, or maybe dog — pierced to play
A three-note tune before Pizarro's day;
Stout and bearded, in the artists's likeness,
A glazed philosopher; two netsukis
Carved minutely, the fissures browned with age —
Jovial traveller, child upon his back,
Shifty rogue sprawled across an oyster-shell —
Jacket fastenings for some mandarin
They survived their function to tell a tale.

Telephone rings, harsh-peremptory,
World is breaking in.
"Hello. Bad news, I'm afraid. Hugh is dead."
Empty sounds struggle with empty space.
He was forty-six, climbing last weekend,
Coronary thrombosis, so they said.

The dog is asleep, the fire burned low,
Cold creeps under the door.
From the mantelshelf
Leers the pre-Columbian artefact.
Quick, quick, fling on logs,
Poke the embers,
Make a blaze.
Bowed beneath his burden,
Barrel-bellied Chinaman laughs out loud.

# BETWEEN HEAVEN AND EARTH (1983)

Given a choice of the better known mountains of North Wales, I always make for the Carneddau. However busy the season, there is room enough for everyone. Here, the hills can swallow the crowds and still retain their dignity. I tend to think of them as rolling, grassy mountains which is, of course, not strictly true.

The glaciated backwalls of Cwm Dulyn, Craig yr Ysfa and Ysgolion Duon (Black Ladders) are as steep and fierce as any, while the three highest summits — Pen yr Oleu Wen, Carnedd Dafydd and Carnedd Llewelyn — are connected by a rocky ridge and boast their fair share of scree. But north of Llewelyn the ridge broadens to a plateau and, with the exception of that striking, but easily skirted, little mountain Tal y Fan, the grasslands stretch all the way to Conwy.

For some, this is boring country. But for me it is a region where the stride lengthens, the spirit lifts, and the eyes are freed to roam over Anglesey, far out to sea, and across the broad green rift of the Conwy Valley to the Denbigh moors beyond. It is not a dramatic landscape but it has a spaciousness missing from most Welsh mountains. It is a big area, twelve miles or more as the crow flies from Ogwen to Conwy, with scarcely a track in between, and eight miles from Bethesda across to Dolgarrog. Yet its spaciousness owes something, also, to the lack of surrounding mountains, for this is the northern extremity of the Cambrian Chain, and to the special magic wrought when sea and mountains meet.

In summer, the Carneddau are a fell runner's delight, especially the firm turf of the prehistoric trackways encircling Tal y Fan. In winter, you must travel far to find a more exhilarating day on skis than the traverse of the Carneddau from north to south. At all times, they are magnificent walking, but their nature is such that they respond particularly well to an informal approach. I have precious memories of pre-dawn starts, of a moonlit crossing of the range, and of sitting entranced on top of Yr Elen as colour faded from the western sky, lights came on in Bethesda and Beaumaris, and night crept up the valley towards us.

One of my favourite ways up onto the Carneddau is from the ash and alder woods of Aber where Llewelyn the Last and his brother Dafydd once held court. Overcome by the Normans, the two princes achieved immortality on the summits. A path climbs steadily up the left flank of the valley, crossing screes and slabs to rejoin the river just above Aber Falls. The falls are a tremendous sight after heavy rain, though best seen from the valley bottom. Not far above is an elaborate cellular fold used by shepherds for sorting sheep. I used to think it a bomb-proof camp site till the autumn night when a gale came screaming down from the tops and hurled itself upon our tents. Ignoring the resistance offered by stone walls, it snapped two ridge poles, tore a flysheet apart, and sent us, sodden and bedraggled, on our way at first light. Beyond the fold, a faint path follows the twist and turns of the river, over grassy flats where ponies often graze and past deep pools that speak of idyllic summer afternoons. The stream finally peters out into a boggy hillside leaving you to climb up onto Foel Fras, or to pick your way rightwards onto the ridge of Yr Arig with its miniature castles of frost-splintered rock. On a Saturday morning at the beginning of June, this is the route taken by two or three hundred sweating runners in the 1000 metre Peaks Race, on their way from the sea shore at Aber to the summit of Snowdon (the record is three and a half hours). Usually, however, the only signs of life are pipits, sheep, and maybe a few wild ponies.

These ponies roam all over the Carneddau, as they have done since time out of mind. Nevertheless, they are all owned by local farmers and once a year the foals are rounded up to be sold as riding ponies for children. But for the rest of the year, whatever the weather, they run free. A few years ago I found one dead on the east side of the wall that crosses Foel Fras. Returning a fortnight on, the carcass was a seething mass of maggots. When I next visited the place, some months later, there was nothing left but the bones. Now, not even they are to be seen.

That wall across the summit of Foel Fras, with offshoots running eastward for miles down towards the Conwy Valley, is a reminder that there are no such walls on the Aber side of the mountain. Aber is one of the few place in Wales, or Britain for that matter where grazing rights are still held in common. The Enclosure Acts of the last century divided up the common land of many parishes between the freeholders, or landowners, at the expense of those who leased their land. Ostensibly, the Acts were intended to encourage agricultural improvements — drainage, crossbreeding, new strains of crop, and so on — and thus increase productivity, by giving private enterprise its head. In practice, more often than not, they increased the wealth of the wealthy, while depriving the poor of a place to graze their animals and collect firewood or peat. That there was not quite the mass exodus from the land that accompanied the clearances in Scotland was due to the development of slate quarries and copper and lead mines in the same period. Be that as it may, one of the few stipulations of the Parliamentary Commissioners was that owners should enclose their new lands. In lowland Britain, the result was thousands of miles of hawthorn hedges. In the uplands, the legacy of Enclosure was a network of beautifully built walls, still crucially important to many hill-farmers, yet all too easily broken down by thoughtless walkers.

If you walk from Snowdon over all fourteen of the Welsh 3000 ft. peaks, Foel Fras is the last to be visited. One November evening, having completed the Fourteen Threes on my own, I was careering in the dark down the steep grass slope that leads to Drum. It had been a dry but cold day, the rocks glazed by the first frost of the winter. Suddenly, without warning of any kind there was a flash of lightning and, simultaneously, a tremendous clap of thunder. To my dying day, I shall remember the shock of that moment, caught in mid-stride, transfixed. More lightning followed, illuminating the mountains like a cosmic flash-gun, and for five minutes I squatted on the hillside below Drum till the storm moved away.

On Drum itself there is an imposing cairn, a massive pile of stones bigger than any summit monument built by walkers. All the way along the spine of the range there are more of these huge cairns, on Foel Grach, Llewelyn, Dafydd and on the col just before Pen yr Oleu Wen. The name Carneddau is derived from them and excavation has shown them to be Bronze Age burial sites, at least 3000 years old. Their presence is not so extraordinary when one recalls that at that time Britain was enjoying a climate far warmer and drier than it is now. The settlement below Llyn Dulyn, which is probably of the same age, is 1600 ft. above sea level; and on both east and west sides of the mountains, the strip of land between the 800 ft. and 1400 ft. contours is rich in prehistoric remains — cairns, cromlechs, circles and standing stones. There are few occupied houses that high in Wales today. Trees, oak and birch especially, would have grown to a height not attained by even the hardiest of the Forestry Commission's imported conifers. But the tops would still have been bare, and it is not difficult to imagine herdsmen ranging far and wide with their sheep and cattle, just as they do in the Himalayas. It would have been natural for these people to bury their leaders on the summits. A love for mountains may be a relatively recent phenomenon, but a reverence for them as places that are "between heaven and earth" seems to have been instinct in man from the earliest times.

As you descend from Drum beside an Enclosure wall to the standing-stones of Bwlch y Ddeufaen (Pass of the Two Stones) and follow the Roman road down towards the sea, only the least imaginative can fail to feel themselves inheritors. True, the landscape has been hideously disfigured by the 20th century's contribution, a double column of jackbooted pylons that goose-step their way across the Carneddau at this point. But pylons cannot destroy the overwhelming sense of a human past in these mountains, a continuity of life and work that mocks any attempt to call it a wilderness area, but makes it no less valuable for that. Descending a sunken lane back into the woods and flowers of the Aber Valley, beneath an Iron Age hill fort, you are taking a route used, no doubt, by Neolithic shepherds, Bronze Age traders, Roman legionnaires and Welsh guerrillas. It is a past worth cherishing.

# A CWM EIGIAU CIRCUIT (1982)

Cwm Eigiau is a favourite stamping ground of mine. I remember, one grey, mid-November day, picking my way up the steep, wooded hillside behind Dolgarrog. It was a long approach to Carnedd Llewelyn, but to walk from a tidal river is to appreciate fully the height of a mountain second only to Snowdon; and to start from the valley floor is to feel more keenly the bleakness of a plateau where freeze-thaw activity is still sorting loose stones into stripes and polygons.

Where the angle eases, beech and oak give way to bracken, thorn trees and old field systems. The slope is dotted with ruins whose occupants gave up the unequal struggle with wind, rain, and poor soil, and departed for the cities or the colonies. No-one actually lives here now. 'You cannot live in the present, at least not in Wales', wrote R.S. Thomas. In this lonely upland, which is possibly emptier than it has been for 4000 years, you can understand what he meant. Our century's contribution to this landscape is less poignant — a hideous black pipe line that carries water from Llyn Cowlyd to the hydro-electric power station in Dolgarrog. I ducked under the pipe and climbed up onto the broad spur which gives a long, rough haul up Pen Llithrig-y-wrach. A peregrine passed overhead, flying fast and determined towards the cliffs of Creigiau Gleision. Miles away to the south, a lake on Moel Siabod glittered in the grey landscape. Clouds were gathering in the west, the wind was stronger, up here, and cold. Rain could not be far away, but on the Great Orme, as usual, the sun was shining.

From the summit, I ran down the grassy slope to Bwlch Tri Marchag, the pass of the three horsemen, where three parish boundaries meet. Easy to imagine three dignitaries, back in history, leading their horses to this spot, perhaps to settle a dispute, and giving the place a name for evermore. Less easy, though, to find a source for Pen Llithrig-y-wrach, the slippery slope of the witch.

A short, steep climb leads to the top of Pen yr Helgi Du. It is a spacious summit, but a few steps northwards bring a dramatic change. Abruptly the ridge narrows to a knife-edge, revealing for the first time the dark waters of Ffynnon Llugwy on the one hand, and the ruins of the Cwm Eigiau slate quarries, derelict since 1890, far below on the other. Almost simultaneously the ridge plunges downwards, confronting one with the huge craggy profile of Craig yr Ysfa, and though it soon becomes apparent that the descent is a short one, it is steep and hands are needed in places. At the col, a zigzag path up loose scree arrives from

Ffynnon Llugwy. Since the CEGB, with arrogant disregard for the purpose and meaning of a National Park, built a tarmac road up to the lake in the early seventies, this path has become so popular that it has had to be repaired with ugly, gabian cages (wire boxes filled with stones).

A short scramble up a rock slab from the col leads to Craig yr Ysfa, really a shoulder of Carnedd Llewelyn rather than a top. Three of the classic rock climbs of Snowdonia emerge hereabouts — Amphitheatre Buttress, Pinnacle Wall, and Great Gully. There were three climbers on the upper arête of the former, their small figures adding scale to the surrounding rock.

A few feet short of the summit of Llewelyn I peered over the edge on my right, where scree slopes drop steeply to Ffynnon Llyffant, a rarely visited little tarn surrounded by aircraft debris. Horrifying numbers of aircraft crashed in these mountains during the last war when inexperienced aircrews lost their way in bad weather. In the hard winter of '78 I had stood in this same spot nervously contemplating a steep snow slope, pondering on the 'lonely impulse of delight' that had brought me there on ski. Then I had found myself, almost without thinking, launching out into the first turn. Today, Snowdon was buried in cloud and the wind was biting. Hands thrust deep in pockets, I passed quickly over the summit to a view of Anglesey, Puffin Island, and a wide expanse of sunlit sea. Just before the grassy plateau between Llewelyn and Foel Grach, I turned aside to investigate the small rock tower that is a conspicuous feature from the east. All around it are loose stones originally piled up by men, and on its top the remains of a circular burial cairn. Legend has it that this was the resting place of the Tristan or Tristram of the Arthurian stories; but it was probably old before Arthur's time, dating, like the other large cairns up here from the Bronze Age.

From the plateau, I turned away down the broad ridge that runs southeast to a region of eroding peat hags overlooking Dulyn and Melynllyn — deep, dark lakes overhung by wet, vegetated crags which house a rich flora safe from the depredations of sheep or people. Downstream of Dulyn, the walled enclosures of the Bronze Age settlement stood out clearly. Behind me, wraiths of cloud were swirling about Llewelyn and, suddenly, the steep, glaciated faces I had just traversed became an inky black, the pale, grassy flank of Pen Llithrig standing out like snow by contrast.

Turning, I ran the length of the ridge to the ruined farm of Tal-y-llyn, drops of rain chasing me down the wind. As the light faded, I sped along a narrow road and down the steep footpath beside the Dolgarrog gorge. Its waterfalls and pools, familiar from playful summer afternoons, glinted sombrely in the gloaming. It was dark by the time I reached the car.

# Climbing with a Difference

# NIGHT OUT (1971)

"Night climbing, sir? No, there's none of that now, sir. It's all demonstrating and smashing things nowadays." And the elderly porter shook his head regretfully.

David hadn't done King's and it was his last night in Cambridge. Gloomily he remarked that he was 'going out with a whimper'. The remedy was obvious.

David's poncho bulging strangely, we scrunched noisily over the gravel towards the chapel, the din of three May Balls reverberating about us. If only the fifteenth-century sculptor knew how useful the tail of that dog would be! Might be dangerous to swing on it, though. Up the glass, just like a ladder, till half way up there's a tug on the rope. Two voices below. A splashing sound, and one voice remarks that there will be a bare patch in the grass next year. Once before, at that same spot, I had looked through a hole in the glass to see torch-beams flashing inside. Fortunately the Dean mislaid the key to the roof. The voices move away and there is a wide step across into the corner. A stone bracket provides a thread runner. The drainpipe is square, with its sides flush to the wall. Finger-tips and friction, but plenty of resting places — curious how, in the dark, you feel yourself to be falling backwards even when in balance — and at the top a gorgeous metal jug on which to swing, heave, mantelshelf, before crawling through an embrasure.

David started to climb. The throbbing beat of the Stones would drown anything, I thought. Immediately, the sharp metallic clink of a karabiner rang out like a gunshot. I glared over the edge, but could only make out a vague shape a long way below. The dew on the roof was soaking through my trousers. Too bad. Stars, hold your fires... Where are they, though? Hell, it's getting light already. Come on, David. A head appeared suddenly and David squeezed through the hole, panting.

The pinnacles are easy enough, the spikes no more than a nuisance. Though, pulling up on one crenellation, two foot square, I found that it was coming away in my arms. Hastily, I pushed it back and grabbed something else. Summits can be places for meditation, but there was no time on this one. On the Fellows' lawn the first blackbird was awake. David climbed up and down again, and we prepared to abseil back to the vestry roof. As I started to descend, David touched my sleeve. "How do you abseil?" he whispered.

Five minutes later we were leaning over Garret Hostel Bridge watching the May Ball couples punting their way to Grantchester. A policeman approached quietly and leant beside us. David hitched his poncho a little closer. "Morning, officer." "Lovely morning," was the affable reply. We strolled away. An owl floated down the lane ahead of us. Behind, the archaic rhythms were pulsating still, but in the clear cold morning light, the chapel stood austerely aloof.

# ROCK AND RUN (1993)

I was near the top of Scafell, soaked to the skin and not warm. The showers of the previous hours had settled to a heavy, persistent rain which was cascading down the gully in little waterfalls. Although it was the end of May, my fingers were numb. My feet, in Walsh running shoes, were numb too, and skating about on the greasy rock. It was growing dark, there was perhaps half an hour to nightfall. I realised that this could not be Broad Stand, but on the other hand, I had no torch and there was not enough time to descend and find the right way. It had to be up.

By this time, I was sixty metres above the screes at a bulging constriction. The only feasible route was out of the gully — more of a chimney by now — to the right. I made a long step across to straddle the gap, trusting my feet not at all on flat slippery ledges. Then I needed a handhold to pull myself across but nothing seemed quite positive enough for frozen fingers. Yet to retreat from here would not only be difficult but would mean benightment. I lurched across with a heave and a prayer and scrambled up into a grassy haven.

There was no going back now. But I quickly realised that the difficulties were far from over. With more than a hint of panic, I tried first a greasy slab on the right, then a steep corner on the left, liking the look of neither. The likelihood of a bivouac crossed my mind, but it did not bear contemplating. I was dressed in trackster bottoms, a t-shirt and a thin sweater, under a lightweight cag that ceased to be waterproof years ago. I had been running thirteen or fourteen hours in a circuit of the lakeland fells. I had no food left in my bum-bag. I would be hypothermic in minutes, let alone hours, if I stopped moving.

Settling for the slab, I found myself poised on small holds, with little of relevance for my fingers and no faith at all in the studded soles of my shoes. One leg started to shake. I was conscious of gloomy space beneath me. I was frightened, and angry at getting myself into such a situation. Before my foot could be shaken off, I made the stretch upwards, right hand settling on a rounded hold just as my left foot shot off. The hold was not enough. Both knees scrabbled on the slab giving just enough purchase for the fingers of my left hand to claw into a tuft of grass. Heart thumping, I hauled myself up.

No time to waste. Stumbling on into the gloaming I emerged onto the upper slopes of Scafell to meet the full blast of a gale. Quickly, I visited the summit and returned a few yards to where a small path dropped down the other side of the ridge. The map I had borrowed had been trimmed at the 600 metre contour and I had to assume that downwards would lead to Wasdale. Scree soon turned to grass, and even after I had lost the path I was able to continue running through the dark. Once, I nearly tripped over a startled fox. Eventually, I hit a stony track running beside the boundary wall of some woodland. Civilization could not be far away. Finally, the dim glow of an interior light loomed up ahead and, with relief, I joined Alan and Joy Evans in the warmth of their little car, where they had been waiting some time. Every so often, a violent gust would rock it alarmingly. The rain beat on the windows. Without regret, I called off my attempt on the Bob Graham round.

Fell running is what you make it. It can be just a branch of athletics; equally, it can be a form of mountaineering as rewarding as any other. For me, it provides a greater sense of personal freedom than either hill-walking or roped climbing, and it need not be lacking in adventure ...

Walkers have always been a little scornful of runners for their cavalier treatment of the hills. You can't see much of your surroundings, they argue. And it is true, you don't notice much except the stones at your feet when you are grinding up to Bochlwyd or skipping from rock to rock over the Glyderau. But perception can be intensified by fatigue and views are all the more wonderful for the effort expended. Striding out over the turf of the northern Carneddau or bounding down the long ridge that leads from Moel Siabod to the Pen y Gwryd, I, for one, know a delight and an exuberance rarely felt at other times. Sights, sounds, sensations may be absorbed fleetingly, subliminally even, but they have a powerful effect and the bubbling sense of well-being that follows a mountain run goes beyond the merely physical. It is a gladness of spirit, never experienced running on a road, that grows out of the cloud song of skylarks, the casual acrobatics of a raven, the sparkle of rain drops on grass after a shower, the spongy softness of sphagnum underfoot, the rich glowing green of polytrichum moss in evening sunlight, or the sudden clap of wings as terrified pigeons hurtle past, a peregrine in hot pursuit. All those individual strands that make up the texture of a mountain day are amplified by the effort and absorption of running. Much detail in the landscape fabric is missed by passing so swiftly over it, but that which registers has an immediacy and impact unknown to the more sedate traveller. It is more akin to the experience of the climber who may notice the cluster of crystals in a pocket, the tiny fern sprouting from the back of a crevice, the flow-banding in the rock at his feet, but is rarely in a position to linger over them.

One of my favourite ways of enjoying the hills is to combine running with soloing relatively easy climbs. This introduces dramatic changes in pace and focus while demanding even greater concentration. I well remember one outing of this type. It was during a grey, cold spell in October; perfect weather for running, chilly on the fingers for climbing. Starting later than intended on the Amphitheatre Buttress of Craig yr Ysfa, I ran by way of Carnedd Llewelyn and classic climbs on Tryfan, the Idwal Slabs and Glyder Fawr down into the Llanberis Pass. By the time I reached Cyrn Las the autumn day was drawing to a close. I had run many miles and climbed 2500 ft of rock. All went well, however, until that point near the top of Main Wall where it becomes necessary to move left round an arête onto a steep wall overhanging a deep, dark gully. It must be one of the most exposed pitches in Wales. As I stepped round my fingers reached that degree of cold when it is hard to tell whether they have a firm grip or not, when even large holds do not feel quite large or incut enough. For several minutes I was uncomfortably aware that there was not another soul in Cwm Glas, night was drawing in, there were hundreds of feet of air beneath me, and I did not relish down-climbing what I had come up. Finally, I made the moves. Adrenalin propelled me up the rest of the climb and onto Crib-y-Ddysgl, where gravity took over and I jogged contentedly down the Zig-Zags to Glaslyn. I was weary, but acutely conscious of my surroundings, so familiar and yet so strange: the silent, empty cwm, a yellow, rising moon reflected in the dark water of the lake, and Snowdon hulking hugely overhead. I slept well that night.

Of course, not every excursion has to be quite so strenuous, nor does it have to become an epic to be memorable. One of the attractions of both running and soloing is the amount you can do in a short space of time. It is possible, for example, to squeeze in a climb, or a mountain, or both, before breakfast ...

Early one summer's morning, when mist was rising from the edges of the Mymbyr Lakes and the reflection of the Snowdon Horseshoe was marred only by the dimples of rising trout, I left the car at Pen-y-Pass and jogged sleepy-legged up to Lliwedd. A red sky in the west and a lurid yellow light from the rising sun were soon smothered by grey stratus, with a few sinister lenticulars hanging beneath, like zeppelins, that boded no good. No matter, I would be up and away before the weather broke.

There was no-one about but a few indifferent sheep and a pair of noisy ravens. The grass was bright with specks of colour: yellow tormentil, blue milkwort, pink lousewort — strange names but much-loved, inseparably associated with summer in the hills. On the crag, bell-heather was in bloom, the bilberries not yet ripe. The rock was dry after a long spell of fine weather and warm to the touch from the early sun. The climbing, nearly a thousand feet of it, was a delicate delight, sloping holds for the feet, pinch-grips for the fingers. It would be a nightmare in the wet. I referred to the guidebook once or twice, for lines on Lliwedd are not obvious and it is easy to climb into difficulties. But most of the time I simply followed holds well-worn by the nailed boots of previous generations. I felt myself the inheritor of Archer Thompson and Winthrop Young and thought of that day when Mallory dislodged a boulder near the top, setting off an avalanche that gave the route its name.

I emerged onto the summit to be startled by demonic shrieks and roars from Cwm y Llan far below. Then the penny dropped: shepherds were gathering the sheep for shearing. On Bwlch y Saethau, the Pass of the Arrows, where Arthur fought his last battle they say, a man was leaning on his crook, shouting to his dogs. I bade him good morning and received a perfunctory nod in return. I was not surprised. Welsh farmers, unlike their Lakeland counterparts, have never seen mountains as anything more than grazing land, and regard any other activity upon them with an attitude that varies from amused indifference to angry contempt. But then, both their language and their way of life are sore-pressed these days. Perhaps a defensive attitude is inevitable. I shrugged resignedly and ran on up the steep screes of the Watkin Path, not much faster than walking, probably, but good for legs and lungs I tell myself. And so to the highest point in England and Wales where, as yet, all was quiet.

Way below, the water of Llydaw and Teryn and the distant Mymbyr lakes glinted in the grey-blue mistiness, enfolded by the arms of Moel Siabod and the Glyderau. In the east, too, lakes were the only features to stand out from the enveloping haze — silver reflections up on the Moelwyns, around Manod, and farthest of all, little Llyn Conwy set in the boggy heath of the Migneint. A one-legged herring-gull cocked its head hopefully but I had nothing to give it. Over the airy crests of Crib-y-Ddysgl and Crib-Goch I ran with care, making it a point of honour to balance along the knife edge, then, stride lengthening, down the path and back to Pen-y-Pass. I glanced at my watch. It was exactly three hours since I had left the car. There was time for a quick cup of coffee in Capel Curig before starting work. Rain was in the air, the best of the day was over. But I did not mind. I had made the most of it and in my pocket was a keepsake, a small but perfect crystal from one of the stony ledges of Lliwedd.

# *Wintertime*

# POINT FIVE (1973)

I looked at my watch — it was only nine o'clock. What could have woken me so early? Then I became aware of Geoff regarding me sleepily. "I know what that bloke meant," he mumbled, "when he said that if you are dry you can't possibly imagine being wet." That seemed an odd thing to say, but it was too much of an effort to think of a reply, so I just grunted. Only gradually did it all come back, culminating in that eternal, 20 mph, lay-by-crawling drive, and our arrival five hours before, stumbling up the streaming hillside to the bothy. Dreamily, I luxuriated in the knowledge that we really were dry and warm.

A wet cold had been the dominant sensation all day. The sploshing, boot-sucking walk up through the peat from the distillery at midday had been normal — the wet feet part, anyway. It was normal, too, that the back of my shirt should be soaked with sweat from the sack, even though the forecast had been for a low freezing level. But the stance at the foot of the first pitch beneath overhanging rock which perpetrated a myriad drips that did not quite add up to a waterfall, seemed out of place on a Scottish winter climb where, as all the best books tell you, weather of arctic ferocity can be expected. I had a waterproof jacket, but that nasty clammy feeling was soon advertising itself around my neck, working its way insidiously downwards, and my breeches drank up the moisture like thirsty cacti.

But if I was damp on the stance, I wasn't going to become any drier by climbing. I was safely to one side of the spindrift cascades that were being flushed almost incessantly down the gully: Geoff was right under them, and every so often he would disappear completely. Then, the two ropes vanishing into mobile whiteness were the only assurance that I was not entirely alone. I was reminded of that wet day a fortnight previously, when we had walked as far as the CIC intending to do this climb, thought better of it, and done battle with a rainy Clachaig Gully instead. Not that I was watching closely, for chunks of ice, large and small, and some very large, were peeling off the rock above and all around, rattling like castanets on our helmets, and it was asking for trouble to look up. They weren't as lethal as stones, but the whirring and whining and banging kept me in a state of expectant, hunched-up tension. But then, I was not climbing.

When Geoff had traversed left across a steep wall and disappeared back right over a bulge, and it was my turn to climb, I discovered that I no longer had time to worry about the lumps of ice. When the big flows came, I could only take a deep breath, keep my head down and cling on for dear life; and when the deluge eased, the sleeves of my jacket would be filled with snow, because it doesn't have storm-cuffs. I would look up quickly to spot the next few moves, only to find that snow had piled up behind my glasses and I was blind. I was shivering and uncoordinated, and my hands lacked strength to grip the hammers. No, there wasn't time to worry about falling ice.

I was still cold when I reached Geoff. It hadn't seeped through to him yet, and as I wrung out the dripping Dachsteins, grumbling, he said with just a hint of malice, "This'll warm you up." I glanced surreptitiously upwards, and caught a glimpse of an alarmingly vertical ice groove before the next torrent arrived. "We must be crazy," I remarked, and started climbing. Perhaps we were, perhaps we should have abseiled off. The climb was manifestly 'out of condition' and we hadn't started it till 2.30pm. But it's good to be crazy sometimes. When I lose the urge occasionally to flout the rules, to laugh in the face of the pundits, I shall know that mental middle-age has set in and it is time to be measured for my coffin. Besides, now that I was leading, and all energy and attention were about to be absorbed to the exclusion of wet and cold and mere physical sensation, retreat was the last thing on my mind.

Technically, the pitch was hard, but easier than it looked, because often it was possible to bridge and not many moves were properly out of balance. Just as well, since it was like climbing Mr. Whippy ice-cream. Only occasionally did the hammer picks bite in securely, and since I could have waited all day for the spindrift to stop, most of the time I had no idea where I was placing hands and feet. Once, the snow gave way beneath me, and, as the weight came on my arms, the hammer picks sliced out. Even as I registered that I was falling off, both feet relocked into a bridging position two feet lower down.

Normally, I suppose, I would have been left quivering with fright. But the bombardment of ice and near-suffocation in rushing drift rendered thought impossible and I was quite unmoved. Geoff hadn't noticed — only the blue top of his crash-hat was visible below — and I reflected that 'what the eye don't see the heart don't grieve over'. Banging in an ice-peg, more because it seemed the right thing to do than because I believed in it, I moved up again, and before long was ensconced in a little bay where I could rest and place a proper peg runner.

Above was a steep chimney but it seemed straightforward by comparison, and a chimneying position, with immovable rock to brace my back against, felt deliciously safe. The notorious final pitch was rearing up ahead now, and hoping to belay on rock at the foot of it, I started up another, easier-angled chimney. Halfway up, however, the rope came tight and I had to search for a belay. On ice you either climb a steep pitch quickly or you fall off: it is the quest for protection that takes time. It took me longer to find a crack that would accept half an inch of inverted blade than to climb the pitch, and though voices stood no chance against the continual hurly-burly of the snow, I was conscious of misery down below. Finally I was tied on and, wedging myself into the chimney, yanked the rope for Geoff to come.

I was a long time in that position, because Geoff knackered himself taking out the ice-peg and had to be lowered down for a rest. It was sleeting wetly and there wasn't much to look at in the confines of the chimney. In such a situation, between bouts of shivering, one cannot help but ponder. I thought back to that perfect weekend earlier in the winter, when there had been queues for all the famous gullies, and from high on Observatory Buttress I had counted sixteen climbers clustered on the Great Tower. It had been a marvellous weekend of firm snow and brilliant sunshine, yet anti-climax had hovered over it. The summit of the Ben had been as populous as the top of Matlock High Tor on a summer's afternoon. Somehow, it just wasn't winter climbing. This was less enjoyable; in fact, I can't pretend that I enjoyed a single moment of the day, in the way that one consciously savours sunny stances and warm rock, or eating steak and chips. But so what? What mattered was that the door of the CIC was locked in silent condemnation and we had the mountain to ourselves. Despite clothes that clung as though I had fallen into a swimming pool, and teeth that chattered like a pneumatic drill, I was glad to be there. That sounds like bullshit, I know. I can only insist that it was true. Admittedly, morale reached an all-time low when, after an hour, Geoff was still on the stance below. I even went so far as to suggest an abseil, but a timely gust of wind blew the words to the oblivion they deserved, and almost immediately the rope started coming in again.

Finally Geoff arrived, looking as uncomfortable as I felt, with pendulous drips on eyebrows and nose, but stoical as ever. His hands were still very cold, so I led on. The final pitch looked ferociously steep, and by the time I was forty feet from the stance and a nut runner had lifted out, confidence demanded a couple of ice screws. The top one popped out when I tested it, but there didn't seem to be any firmer ice, so I pushed it back in and pretended not to notice. In fact, this pitch also proved bridgeable, and it was legs rather than arms that could do the work; otherwise, handholds might have been necessary, as the hammer picks just weren't biting. Unexpectedly soon I reached the top, emerging to a blessed region where spindrift flowed past my feet instead of over my head. Above, the gully lay back at a comfortable angle for two hundred feet or so, before the mist gobbled it up. I felt like yodelling, but my mouth was too dry, so I simply grinned to myself, and then at myself, and was happy.

As usual, the belay was poor, but Geoff didn't come onto the rope, and soon we were moving together up into the gathering gloom, wondering if we could be off the mountain before dark. We had forgotten the cornice. If we had been sensible Geoff would have buried his deadman just below it and I could have climbed it in relative safety. But we were both tired, and when I told him not to bother with a belay, he took me at my word and stayed where he was, 100 ft lower. The cornice wasn't *that* big, but the snow was rotten, and twice I was left dangling from a horizontally embedded axe. The second time, my arms felt as though they couldn't take much more. It was no time to worry about margins of safety. Burying one arm in the snow and holding my breath lest the footholds collapse again, I cautiously withdrew the axe and slashed at the lip until I could reach over and tap the axe vertically downwards. Seizing it in both hands, I threw one leg over the top and rolled sideways onto the plateau. We were up.

However, the saga was by no means over. The Ben was wrapped in drizzling mist and night had fallen. It was a cautious, probing descent along the plateau rim to No. 4 Gully. Moisture on my glasses reduced visibility to almost nil, and as I could see even less without them I gratefully abandoned responsibility to Geoff. Once, we thought we were going uphill and turned back, abortively. But in the end we found the marker post and Geoff went over the edge. "Blimey, it's steep," he muttered. "Don't worry" I replied casually, "there'll be plenty of holds." There was an almost inaudible swish, and Geoff had gone. Aghast, I peered over in time to see a dark flailing object come to rest, an inanimate heap, 120 feet below. "Are you all right?" I called inanely, conscious of it even at the time. No reply. Now what? My brain unwillingly began to consider possible courses of action. At that moment the heap stirred, stood up, began to brush itself. Relief almost instantaneously gave way to anxiety as I realised that now it was my turn to climb down. I examined the marker post, hoping for an abseil, but it was inclined and the rope would have slipped off. Reluctantly, I lowered myself into blackness and found what Geoff had found, that there were no ready-made holds in the vertical little head-wall. Having kicked steps for my feet, and thrust in the axe as far as it would go, I was faced with the problem of the next out-of-balance move. Suddenly it was made for me. The footholds collapsed, the axe pulled out, and I was falling free. It was only for a few feet, but when I landed I toppled over backwards, and at once I was rolling and somersaulting out of control. I was never too worried, because the snow was deep and the angle of No. 4 eases off quickly, but I was relieved nonetheless when I slowed to a halt just below Geoff.

There was no more drama after that. Only the long plod down Coire na Ciste, falling through the snow uncaring into meltpools and hidden streams. The CIC had become a seductive dream of warmth and brews, but the reality was still darkly barred. Squelching downwards by the light of a single headtorch, we met a few weekend hopefuls near the dam and complacently filled them with gloom. Midnight. At the old railway line a rising moon brushed aside the clouds to escort us on our way and the sickly aroma of whisky wafted us the last few yards through the distillery. At the car, the bliss of dry clothes — and the rude shock of a syphoned petrol tank. Finally, the long, long crawl round the loch to the Coe, Geoff waking periodically with a jerk of wheel, worried lest he break his car yet again.

Rain was still pattering on the bothy roof. Geoff was snoring gently. I snuggled deeper into the warmth of my pit.

Looking south from Carnedd Llewelyn

Kings College Chapel, Cambridge, taken by moonlight with an exposure of several minutes.

Carn Etchachan (L) and Shelter Stone Crag (R) from across Loch Avon

Guiding on an alpine voie normale - the Roche Faurio south-east ridge in the Ecrins massif.

Geoff Cohen climbing a steep pitch low down on the Charmoz north face.

Gwyn Davies and The Ladies.

Taking a break in Alaska.

John Cousins trying to make sense of the map in the Tien Shan; Kirov Peak behind.

Geoff Cohen at a bivouac site in Kishtwar.

Dick Isherwood with a long-awaited cup of chang after descending from Annapurna II.

Bob Ferguson posing for a Mars bar in the Alps.

David Gundry after a climb in Cornwall.

Looking down the West Fork glacier from an unnamed peak in the Hayes Range, Alaska.

Dick Sykes emerging from an Italian bivouac hut.

Dick Renshaw at the top of the ice-field on the north face of the Droites.

Malcolm MacArthur and Elphine on board the RRS Brensfield.

Netti Collister the morning after emerging from the Hidden Valley.

First view of the peak Parbati South, 6128 m, in Kulu, seen from the col of 5150 m on the approach from the Sainj valley.

Thui II, Chitral, from the north.

Rob Ferguson and Dave Wilkinson studying Mehrbani from the top of Snow Dome, Naltar valley, Gilgit.

Descending the Sat Marao glacier, Gilgit.

Mike Browne coping with a recalcitrant stove at high altitude.

David Williams - the worse the snow , the better he skis.

Rob Wood at the helm.

Laurie Wood & Skookum aboard the Quintano.

John Pirquet having a dip before breakfast in the wilds of Vancouver Island.

# SCORPION (1983)

A fading February day, gloomy greyness merging imperceptibly into night. A lonely building overlooking a bleak, windswept moorland; at its back, snow wraiths disappearing up a dark heather hillside into cloud. A dim light glows from the only window. Inside, the candle gutters in a draught. Pine logs blaze and spit in the open hearth, throwing dancing shadows on the wall but adding little warmth to the bare room. On a bench before the fire, two figures sit, the chill at their backs recalling the merits of old, high-backed settles ...

Down in Glenmore, we had stepped off the bus the day before to find no room in the inn. Shouldering our skis, we had plodded two miles up the little valley through open stands of Scots pine, surprising a group of stags on the strath near the green lochan. Picking up some dead branches we had continued to the bothy, relieved to find it empty. Now, after a day on the congested, icy runnel that was passing for a piste on Cairngorm, we had had enough of skiing and were planning a climb. Netti had used axe and crampons in the Alps but had never climbed in Scotland. The obvious place to introduce her to the esoteric pleasures of Scottish ice was a short, accessible climb in one of the northern corries, but from what we had seen in the Cairngorm car park these corries would be only marginally less crowded than the ski slopes. As I enjoy the company of other climbers in the pub but not on the hill, I decided that Carn Etchachan would be a more suitable venue for her initiation. Overlooking Loch Avon, Carn Etchachan is a big crag, a long way from anywhere. Because of its remoteness, at that time (1974) the route I had in mind had had few ascents since it was first climbed by Tom Patey and Richard Brooke in 1954. Moreover, it was a Grade IV, which some would regard as too hard for a first climb. But the name, Route Major, and its associations with the Brenva face on Mont Blanc, seemed to imply that its grade was derived from length rather than difficulty. And to cope with the long approach, we agreed to make an expedition of it.

We left the bothy next morning with bivi gear and two nights' food. There was a bitter wind blowing down Strath Nethy as we toiled up deep drifted snow, tracked only by hare and ptarmigan and a solitary purposeful fox. The view from the Saddle was not inspiring. The cloud base was more than halfway down the crag and there were flurries of snow on the wind. We hurried down to the edge of the frozen loch but thought better of walking across it. Ahead was a jumble of huge boulders fallen from the crags above, among them the famous Shelter Stone, reputed to have accommodation for twelve. We reached it, tired and none too early, only to find it choked with snow. Some energetic digging made it habitable, if not exactly comfortable, for two.

The following morning the wind was stronger, eddying spitefully among the boulders, picking up loose snow and throwing it in our faces as we emerged from the shelter. The cloud was even lower, hovering just above the rock known as The Sentinel at the foot of Castle Gates Gully, which is the dividing line between Carn Etchachan and the even more imposing Shelter Stone Crag. Of our route, there was no sign. At the bottom of the gully we opened the guide book, failed to make anything of the description, and put it away for the duration. Adopting the old-fashioned expedient of following the line of least resistance, we started climbing. On firm snow, with occasional bulges of ice, we worked up and left along a system of ramps, then back right beneath steep rock and up a shallow chimney. Three rope lengths brought us to a major fault running up the crag.

I have a photograph taken at this point, underexposed despite a slow shutter speed and maximum aperture, of a dark figure, blurred by spindrift, emerging from the gloom behind. The fault, or gully, above was hidden in cloud but facing us was a rock wall which guarded entry to it. At first glance this looked impassable. The only line to look remotely feasible was a wide chimney on the right-hand side, but there was an ominous overhang at its top and I approached it without much hope. To my surprise, I found I could bridge the chimney. A pick placed blindly over the top, a mighty pull which was translated by a convulsive heave and flailing legs into a mantelshelf, and I was over the obstacle, panting. Netti followed with a speed which I found at once disconcerting and reassuring. That, as she confessed later, she was motivated solely by a desire to be off the mountain as fast as possible, is beside the point. Nevertheless, I could sympathize. The wind was gusting by turns up and down the gully so there was no escaping the stinging facefuls of drift. Stances were a solitary communion with the cold. The fact that we had by now no idea where we were on the crag added all the tension and uncertainty of a first ascent to the climb. But the way above still looked possible, for the next few feet at least, so I pressed on into the mist.

34

I found myself being forced leftwards across a wall of perfect névé, at an unusually steep angle for snow, the heavy rucksack seeking always to pull me out of balance. We began to sense that the top of the crag was not far away. But now we had also reached the end of the gully. We were in a small bay completely enclosed by steep rock. The only conceivable exit was to the left but even that looked hopeless. The rock was thinly coated with hoar frost and apparently quite without holds. My heart sank. We had long since guessed that we were not on Route Major. Only much later, re-reading the guide, did the significance of this sting in the tail dawn on me; although to be honest, I am still not sure what we were really on. At the time, a retreat down the length of the crag, on a single rope, looked a distinct possibility. Nothing ventured, nothing gained, however, so I balanced precariously up, crampon points on small incuts, till I could go no further. Only six feet above and to my left was a snow slope. So near and yet so far. In that six feet there was nothing, save a vertical crack choked with ice. Legs beginning to shake, I cut out the ice from the crack hoping to find a peg placement. It was blind. In desperation, I hammered an ice-peg into the one surviving lump of ice stuck in the crack. It hit rock after two inches and I tied it off. I glanced down at Netti, belayed to her axe thirty feet below. She was hidden inside her hood, paying out the rope mechanically, her mind, no doubt, far away. I moved up using the peg as a handhold, feet scratching, then catching, on something unseen. Still I could not reach across to the snow. Suddenly I was mantelshelfing on that absurd peg, standing on it, wildly thrusting my axe into the snow only to find it soft, useless. Frantically, I packed the snow into the semblance of a handhold and launched myself sideways onto it. It held; and seconds later I was on firm snow at an easy angle. Trembling, I had to rest on my axe for a minute or two before bringing Netti up. Once again, she followed more easily than I expected and a few minutes later we were on the summit.

There was nothing to see and in the tearing wind damp breeches and mittens froze hard as boards. The rope was a wire, to be folded not coiled. A hasty compass bearing took us off the top and down into Coire Etchachan and, as the wild day drew to a stormy close, crampons still on our feet, we stamped thankfully into the Hutchinson Memorial Hut. A candle was lit, the primus purred obediently. Sitting in the dry heather that covered the floor, I pulled clots of ice, one by one, from my beard. For some reason I did not have a helmet and had been wearing an earband rather than a balaclava. The penalty was a mass of frozen curls which melted now and dripped down the back of my neck. As we sipped, gratefully, the first brew, we were both silent. I did not ask what Netti was thinking, I could guess. It had been a long, hard day, not at all what she had been led to expect. Remorse tempered my elation at completing a route which had taxed me as much as I care to be taxed; but the damage had been done and, even now, she quizzes me suspiciously about my intentions whenever we climb together.

The following day dawned bright and calm. The tops were clear. The long walk back seemed very peaceful and we took our time, basking in the sun when it appeared. From the Fords of Avon, bridged with snow, we could look up the loch to Carn Etchachan. At that distance, it was hard to associate it with the drama and discomfort of the previous day. Not until we were back at Ryvoan did we realize that we had not seen a soul for three days.

# The Alps

# EARLY DAYS (1988)

August is not the best of months to climb in British hills. It could aptly be called The Month of the Midge. Let the wind drop, or the sun sink behind a shoulder of the mountain, and up and down the western seaboard of Britain a cloud of midges will appear on cue. Insect repellent is no answer, for it merely drives the creatures down your shirt, up your trouser legs or, worst of all, into your hair. Midges are a potential problem all summer, but in August they seem to reach an annual peak of ferocity and resilience. It is an obvious time to migrate, and if there are midges in the Alps, I have yet to be troubled by them.

By convention, the alpine year is neatly segmented. July and August are for climbing; April and May are for ski-touring; winter lasts from 21 December to 21 March. In between is limbo. Of course, that is nonsense. You can climb in the Alps at any time of year, and if you like a bit of adventure, you may actually prefer to do so out of season. Be that as it may, when I started climbing everyone went to the Alps in August, so I went to the Alps in August; and since everyone seemed to go to Chamonix, I, too, went to Chamonix. In fact, we were four, and because we all climbed VS at Stanage and in Wales, we had a high opinion of ourselves. For our debut we chose the Forbes Arête on the Chardonnet, which we thought rather beneath us for its technical difficulties are negligible, but it would be useful training and acclimatisation. In the event we discovered that, despite a few days in Scotland the previous March, we were not very competent on snow or ice, some of us were not at all fit, and though we knew we should move together most of the time on the rock, in practice it did not feel as safe as we would have liked. In short, we were a fairly typical party of British novices and as a result, like many before us, we were benighted. There was a violent thunderstorm during the night and it snowed heavily. Mick Guilliard had a polythene bag; the rest of us put on our cagoules, stuck our feet in our rucksacks and sat it out. We were frightened and miserable. Next day, after a harrowing (and unnecessary) jump from the lip of a bergschrund, we descended to the valley somewhat chastened.

Our next climb, a short rock route on the Moine, was relatively uneventful. Emboldened by this success we decided to try the east face of the Grépon, a much longer rock climb pioneered by Geoffrey Winthrop Young and Joseph Knubel before the First World War. At first all went well, though we did find ourselves climbing grade IV rock in the dark to reach the hut. This was the Rochers Rouges bivouac, an amazing construction attached to the mountain by a web of wire cables, with a view through the floorboards into space. The climbing next day was interesting and technical on firm, rough granite. We managed to find the way with only occasional errors and climbing as two ropes of two ensured that we did not move too slowly. It was beginning to feel as though the summit could not be far away when, out of the blue, disaster struck. Not a natural disaster, like being hit by a stone or struck by lightning but a human one, almost as dire in its consequences. When things are going badly on a climb, often the second is noticeably more optimistic than the leader: "Looks like a good hold a few feet above you," or "If you can get across to the right, it looks a doddle," and so on. But the converse can also be true, especially on a long climb. While the leader is enjoying the intricacies of route-finding, impelled upwards and onwards by his own momentum, the second has time to look around, to brood and worry. That was what happened on the Grépon. I had reached the top of a pitch, belayed and called "Up you come." There was a pause. Then someone shouted, "Come back down. We've got to retreat." "What?" I was incredulous. "Why?" "The weather's breaking." I looked up the glacier to a few cumulus clouds on the horizon behind the Grandes Jorasses. Even now I do not know quite what induced this panic in the rear. Maybe it was the thought of the Knubel Crack not far above, on which the axe-cling technique, recently re-invented in Scotland as 'torquing', was extensively employed on the first ascent. Maybe the notorious séracs which threaten the descent of the Nantillons glacier had grown preposterously dangerous in the imagination of ignorance. Whatever the reason, I was one and they were three, and they were not coming up. Fuming, but with my head of steam already evaporating, I abseiled down and tried to argue the point. No good. The others were sheepish, but adamant. Down it had to be.

Now abseiling is a lengthy business at the best of times. If you are a party of four, and not very slick at finding anchors, and the knot more than once jams when you pull the ropes down, it is very time-consuming indeed. Before we knew it we were settling down for our second unplanned bivouac in three routes. This time we had a stove and pot so at least we could spend the night brewing up. Alas, someone dropped the pot, so it was cold water after all, and nothing to do but curl up into a foetal position and wait for morning. I had a down jacket, but that did not do much for legs and feet, and the rope only kept out some of the cold seeping up from the rock beneath. Being a clear night it felt, and probably was, colder than our night in the storm, and I made a mental note to buy myself a poly bag. In the morning after a frugal breakfast, we continued on our way. By now we had lost the route of ascent, but we could see the Envers hut below us and were making for that. We had been scrambling down easy rock for a while when we came to a steep gully and set up another abseil from a small rock spike. Mick and John abseiled down, and I followed. Whether the loop slipped off the spike, or the spike itself snapped, I do not know. But one moment I was abseiling down a fixed rope, the next I was attached to nothing, shooting head first, on my back, down the gully. Sideways over a protruding rock I slid, right way up through some soft snow, head first again down a sheet of ice, wondering when something decisive would happen and vaguely registering the faces of Mick and John Hamilton, mouths agape. Suddenly, unexpectedly, I was myself again, stationary, just short of an overhanging rock wall that dropped into a gaping bergschrund. Picking myself up, I brushed some of the snow off my clothes and remarked, "That's one way of getting down, I suppose." Then I felt sick and faint and had to lean against the gully wall.

I had fallen 50 metres with nothing to show for it but a knee which was painful but had not yet begun to stiffen. More serious seemed to be the loss of my ice-axe, which had vanished. The next abseil, when Pete Hughes had climbed down to join us, was, I suppose, therapeutic in the same way as remounting a horse after falling off. But I did not enjoy it one bit. The anchor was a single peg (and we were not very experienced at placing pegs) and the abseil itself was free for the length of the rope, with a pendulum swing at the bottom to reach the lower lip of the bergschrund. Our progress thence down the glacier was slow. The lack of an axe made the snow slopes dangerous and to bend my knee was increasingly painful. Soon I could not bend it at all and was forced to accept that I simply could not walk the whole way down. My first Alpine season ended ignominiously, but not unpleasantly, with a helicopter ride from the Envers hut down to Chamonix.

For reasons I do not understand, instead of putting me off Alpine climbing for good, this inauspicious start made me determined to do better next time. When next I went to the Alps I had three more Scottish winters and two small expeditions to the Hindu Kush behind me. I had learned many lessons in Alpinism the hard way, but having survived them, chiefly by good fortune, I felt far more assured in the mountains. The techniques of travelling on glaciers, moving together on mixed terrain and cutting steps on steep ice all came more naturally. After a fortnight in the Bernina Alps, Rob Ferguson and I felt confident enough to attempt our first *grande course*. We chose the north face of the Grosshorn, an ice climb on the Lauterbrunnen Wall. At that time most major ice routes in the Alps had received very few ascents, and even fewer by British parties. Ice axes with curved or drooped picks had not yet appeared on the market and protection was provided either by long pegs that had to be laboriously chopped out of the ice after use or by ice screws that were more suitable for opening wine bottles than for holding a fall. Everyone talked about front-pointing, but nobody practised it, except on névé.

Rob and I had tried to front-point the Scersen Eisnäse. After 30 ft, discretion proved the better part of valour and we compromised by cutting bucket steps into which we mantelshelfed. British climbers were regarded, and regarded themselves, as rock climbers. Robin Smith's ascent of the Fiescherwand and occasional ascents of the Triolet North face were exceptions that proved the rule. The Dolomites were almost as popular a venue as Chamonix for an Alpine season. In that respect, Rob and I were different. Rob actively preferred ice to rock, while I have always enjoyed rock climbing but am not particularly gifted. On the other hand, week-long sojourns in the CIC hut had made us efficient ice climbers.

Nevertheless, looking back, I am still surprised at our temerity in attempting the Grosshorn. Rob was well-versed in Alpine lore, but in my case I am sure that ignorance was bliss. I had never heard of Welzenbach and was quite unaware of the reputation his climbs had acquired, which was a great advantage. The difficulty of a climb can often lie in the head as much as in the configuration of rock or ice. I once retreated off the Central Pillar of Frêney, in perfect weather, and have regretted it ever since. Ostensibly, we were stopped fairly low down by a pitch we just could not climb. In retrospect I think I was simply fazed by having read Bonatti's account of the harrowing and tragic retreat from that place. My partner, the imperturbable Dick Renshaw, would undoubtedly have worried away until he found a way up or round that pitch, but I was too aware of how high and remote we were, too affected by the historical aura of the place. If reading books can add depth and resonance to the immediate sensations of climbing, it can also make individual climbs much harder. The Eiger with its gruesome, morbidly-documented history, is an extreme example. Even Bonatti failed here to assert mind over matter and retreated from his one solo attempt.

The other difficulty with big Alpine climbs is their appearance. Looked at from straight on, a 50° ice face appears vertical, a rock wall seems sheer and featureless. Experience tells you that ice slopes are rarely as steep as they look, and that close inspection will reveal cracks and flaws in the most compact piece of rock. But it still takes a mental effort, a deliberate stifling of the imagination, first to approach the very foot of a big climb, then to ignore the awful scale of the thing — 1000 metres or more stretching endlessly above — and concentrate on the moves in front of your nose, or at most the line of the next pitch. The need to start as early as midnight to ensure well-frozen snow and to reduce the danger from stones or séracs, is a great help in this respect. One can be well up a face before day breaks, with no need to contemplate it from a distance. In the case of the Grosshorn we were helped even further by a layer of low cloud which, if unpromising for the morrow, at least hid the face from view on our walk up to the Schmadri hut.

Already ensconced in the hut, in fact the only people there, were two other Brits, Dennis Davis and Ray College. We had come to climb one route of several on the Lauterbrunnen Wall, none of which had received a British ascent and yet here was another British party attempting exactly the same route on the same day. We were rather overawed to be in such company: Dennis was a veteran of several Himalayan expeditions and the previous year Ray had climbed The Pear, The Walker and The Eiger in the space of a two-week holiday. They were welcoming and quite uncondescending, however, and we agreed to join forces next day.

After the usual uncommunicative candlelit breakfast, 'each dwelling all to himself in the hermitage of his own mind', we left the hut some time in the small hours, picked a sleepy way over moraines, cramponed up some névés and crossed the bergschrund, always a mental Rubicon, without difficulty. At dawn we were moving together up steepening snow slopes. Shortly afterwards the three of us were belayed to a single tied-off corkscrew, anxiously watching Ray as he methodically chopped his way through the narrows formed by two rock buttresses, on ice only a couple of inches thick. Above stretched 1500 ft of hard ice, demanding steps all the way. As the day wore on we were glad to be four, to share the hard graft of cutting. When not taking our turn at the face, we shifted our weight from one leg to another on small stances, and contemplated the huge sweep of ice above, below and all around, feeling very small and vulnerable. Once, a sudden hostile whirr made us glance round in time to see a single boulder from the upper cliffs bound past a few feet away. It was enough to keep me peering upwards from beneath my helmet, like an anxious tortoise, for the rest of the day. Another cause of uneasiness was the weather. Great clouds were swirling below and sometimes about us. But, fortunately, they never developed into anything serious, and at evening the sky cleared.

Slowly, we chopped our way upwards. As we rose, the sun dropped. The last few hundred feet seemed harder and steeper, interminable: perhaps we were just growing tired. When dark fell, we were still well below the summit but there was no incentive to stop, and we continued doggedly by torch light. My mind was wandering now, feet were cold, legs stiff and aching. It was 10pm before we finally emerged onto the top. We had been climbing 21 hours, climbing characterised more by nervous tension than any technical difficulty. I was aware of chains of light down in the valley. It was August 1st, a Swiss national holiday when children carrying lanterns process through the villages. Our head-torches, we learned later, were taken to be a part of the celebrations. I think the others brewed up; I was too tired to bother. Pulling on my duvet and cagoule, I put my feet into my rucksack, sat on the rope, and fell asleep in a sitting position among some rocks.

There can be few sports in which the distinction between pleasure and happiness is so marked as it is in climbing, particularly climbing in big mountains. Moments of conscious pleasure during the day had been few, moments of discomfort legion. From the torch flashed into my eyes at midnight to the agonising cramp in my calves during that bivouac, there had been suffering of one sort or another. Indigestion, cold, heat, thirst, fatigue and fear had been the dominant sensations of the day. Yet, at the end of it, I was indisputably happy. It was not just relief at a task accomplished, satisfaction at an ambition achieved or anticipation of a limited acclaim. Born of those hours of fatigue, deprivation and stress, in which beauty and grandeur were absorbed almost subliminally, grew an inward singing, which would linger on as a calm content for weeks afterwards. Feelings of regret, sadness, disappointment, seem to be common among mountaineers writing about summit moments, but I have never experienced them. Perhaps my climbs have never been hard enough, or been planned and dreamed about for long enough. All I know is that a taxing Alpine climb leaves me feeling positive about life in general for a long time afterwards. Surely, that is why most of us climb mountains? But there are degrees of happiness. As in so many spheres, the reward is in proportion to the effort expended. In climbing terms, it was some time before I experienced again quite the same high I felt when we awoke to a clear sunny morning on top of the Grosshorn.

Back in the Alps two years later, ice faces seemed suddenly almost straightforward, and everyone was climbing them. Both Chouinard and Salewa were producing axes and hammers with curved picks, designed to penetrate ice rather than shatter it. With such weapons front-pointing became a viable option on the hardest and steepest of ice. Ice climbs could be achieved in fast times even in unfavourable conditions of bare ice rather than névé, yet the leader could feel, and actually was, more secure than when simply standing in steps. Bivouacs, too, had become relatively comfortable with the appearance of the Karrimat. Closed-cell foam had been in use in the States for some years but it only became widely available in Britain after the Annapurna South Face Expedition of 1970. In addition, I had acquired a two-man nylon Zdarski sack, and had decided that a lightweight sleeping bag made more sense than a down jacket weighing the same. Now, so long as we could find room to lie or sit, any bivouac could be a cosy affair.

After several weeks of climbing whenever the weather permitted, on both snow and rock, I found myself fit and confident but temporarily without a partner. I rather welcomed the opportunity to try some climbs on my own. I had few qualms about climbing solo, for a large proportion of all Alpine climbing is unroped or moving together. But to be totally alone on a long climb would be something quite new. I started with the Frendo Spur which went without incident, but there were so many other climbers scattered up and down the route that it did not feel like soloing at all. Next, I decided to try the Route Major on the Brenva Face of Mont Blanc, a long, serious climb but not technically too difficult; and this time I found what I was looking for.

Travelling alone on glaciers is a hazardous business so I was glad to team up with a pair of Norwegians, bound for the Grand Capucin, for the journey across the Vallée Blanche from the Midi. The weather had been poor for some days and I was alone in the Trident hut that night until an Italian guide and his client arrived long after I had gone to bed. They were still asleep when I left just before 1am, tip-toeing thunderously in crampons on the metal walkway outside the hut. The moon was high and almost full, the torch unnecessary as I descended steeply onto the glacier and contoured between some big open crevasses. Col Moore was in shadow, steep and icy but covered with old steps. The Brenva face glowered overhead, but I did not allow myself to contemplate its immensity or the lethal potential of those batteries of séracs up above, and set off on a long rising traverse into the face. At first, the climbing was messy and unpleasant, on loose debris left by a recent rock fall which had spilled down the face, like puke on a drunkard's chin, I remember thinking. Once clear, it was a matter of keeping to the snow, zigzagging through the rock, gaining height but always traversing leftwards. Several times I had to climb down the vertical side of an avalanche runnel deeply scored into the mountain, and up the other side. Once I had to wait a full minute as a torrent of spindrift hissed past. Finally, I recognised the dark mass of the Sentinelle Rouge and climbing the chimney at its side emerged on the edge of the infamous Great Couloir, the main chute for avalanches from the upper regions of the face. I listened hard, took a deep breath, and literally ran across a hundred feet or so of hard but easy-angled water ice. I did not pause until I had scrambled up rocks on the far side and was at last on the ridge crest discovered 40 years before by Graham Brown as the safest line in a dangerous place. There, panting, I stopped and looked around. Way below on the Col Moore, two torches flickered as the Italians set off up the Brenva Spur. I felt separated from them not just by distance but by a gulf of nervous tension. Suddenly, I realised just how frightened I had been of that traverse beneath the séracs. Even in cold conditions, it smacks a little of Russian roulette. Now I found myself actively looking forward to the climbing ahead.

The rock on the spur was nowhere hard but often it was iced and always it demanded attention. The famous snow arêtes came and went, the dark preventing a full appreciation of their position. Climbing rock in bare hands I was aware of the temperature dropping as I gained height and dawn approached. I was fit enough to move fast and continuously and I had to make a conscious effort to relax, to slow down and take in what was around me. I was possessed by a feverish impulse that urged me on, a reaction I suppose to being alone in the dark in such a place. Every now and then I forced myself to stop, to gaze across at the streak of light appearing behind the Diable ridge, the odd flashes of lightning over the Gran Paradiso, or the summit of the Aiguille Blanche where Rob Ferguson and I had sat a few weeks before.

The buttress at the top of the spur was difficult. It was still dark enough to need a torch and the rock was steep. Had I a rope, I would have put it on. As it was, I made do with a long sling threaded through an *in situ* peg as I hauled myself over an ice-coated chock-stone. My first attempts in crampons were unsuccessful and, in the end, I had to take them off and use small incut holds on either side of the chimney. The problem was that I found myself then in an icy gully, in no position to refit the crampons. Acutely aware of 1200 metres of Brenva face stretching away below, I cut steps with the utmost care until the ice ran out and I found myself tip-toeing reluctantly up a verglassed slab.

Now I was beneath the final sérac wall recalling Bonatti's account of pegging up vertical ice. Séracs are never the same from one year to the next, however, and sure enough, there was a way through in which only a short traverse was steep. Above, it was all plain sailing, if hard work through crusted powder. I was glad to find some old tracks which made life easier, and plodded upwards into the dawning day, exulting inwardly if not outwardly. Little more than five hours after leaving the hut, and at the very moment that the sun rose above the horizon, I reached the summit. I pulled on a windproof and sat on my sack to look over valleys filled with blue haze to the Vertes and the Jorasses and beyond to the Grand Combin and the distant peaks of the Valais. I strove to encompass it all and imprint the moment on my memory. Yet I can recall no other details of that view now. It is always the same. It is incidents and random impressions from the ascent that stick in the mind. The views and spectacular surroundings, wonderful though they can be, become merely the matrix for a climb. I always marvel at descriptions by W H Murray and Geoffrey Winthrop Young: they must have trained themselves to be verbal photographers of their surroundings. Yet I do not really regret such failures of memory, or that I took no camera with me that day. For what I do remember is the stillness and inner quiet of those moments, a glimpse of an enviable state of being, all too easily dispelled by the usual chatter of consciousness when one starts fiddling with a camera or writing in a notebook.

Two figures appeared at the other end of the long summit crest. It was time to go. Bubbling with *joie de vivre*, grateful for those few minutes to myself, I ran down the mountainside, past a long, long caravan of despairing, ashen-faced climbers struggling with the altitude. Revelling in health and youth and a comfortable pair of boots, I scorned railway and téléphérique, and by 10.30am was strolling through Chamonix, eating peaches, utterly content, as the clouds of a freak storm swept violently over Mont Blanc.

# GLACIER PATROL (1974)

"Ho, ho, ho," rumbled the elderly guide, escort to a family party on the Haute Route, his laugh loud in an all but empty Schönbiel hut. "Le face nord, peut-être. Ho, ho, ho."

We tried to look as though we had not heard, though grins showed that everybody else had. The cause of the merriment was our desire to leave the hut at midnight. Instead of explaining to the guardian why we wanted to get up at such an unearthly hour, Dick, bashful English gentleman that he is, had only admitted to the half of it. The guardian's amazement on hearing that we were merely skiing to Arolla was understandable. The mad English at it again. But maybe we could not have won, whatever we said. The following afternoon, toiling up the lower slopes of the Rosablanche, when Arolla was a distant memory, we passed two Germans resting on a rock. To the usual questions we answered truthfully that we had left the Schönbiel that morning and intended to be in Verbier that evening. Their reaction was no less incredulous, nay derisory, than the guardian's ...

Yet in their case the incredulity was unjustified. Sometimes called the Glacier Patrol, the route from Zermatt to Verbier is a popular variant on the Haute Route. Usually, it is skied in three or four days, stopping overnight at the Vignettes hut, the Cabane des Dix and sometimes the Cabane Mont Fort. Sections of the Swiss army, however, used to hold an annual race over the route, completing it in a single day, hence the name. This marathon was discontinued after one team had been killed in a crevasse attempting a short cut, but the idea of repeating it had appealed to Dick Sykes for a long time.

Dick, a veteran of Masherbrum and many another foreign range, did not take up skiing till his mid-twenties and with characteristic thoroughness became an instructor before attempting to ski-tour. When he did, he skied the Haute Route three times in his first season. Since then he has skied it solo and was a member of the Alpine Ski Traverse in 1972. In the Glacier Patrol, he saw a test of fitness and stamina uphill, of route-finding ability and safe skiing downhill, and of the efficient interchanging of bindings, skins and crampons that over a long day can save not just minutes but hours. Also, I suspect, he was motivated by a desire to continue the work of the Alpine Ski Traverse in demonstrating that the English *do* know how to use skis in the mountains. As Marcel Kurz, pioneer ski-tourer and prolific Swiss guidebook writer, wrote: "It is a curious fact that the English ... were the first to explore our alps and the last to explore them on ski." While English-speaking climbers have earned for themselves a measure of respect in the Alps, the Briton as ski-tourer is still regarded with some amusement, particularly by the armies of massive, over-equipped Teutons that throng the Haute Route.

For my part, I welcomed the idea of a ski tour that would be physically taxing. Frank Smythe once said: "It took the Himalaya to teach me the delights of mountain travel and I now know that to cross a range by a pass is every whit as enjoyable as climbing a peak." Fair enough; that is what ski-touring is all about after all. But if mountain travel is to be as enjoyable as mountain climbing, it must, in its own way, be equally demanding. As a recent convert to ski-touring, I was enthusiastic about the skiing and the scenery, but hitherto the relative lack of effort involved had left me faintly dissatisfied. The average day lasts only six hours, some of it downhill, the rest in the relaxed rhythm of uphill skinning. Typically, having arrived about midday at a hut, most of the afternoon is slept away and at night Mogodon tablets are swallowed as a matter of course to induce more sleep. Depending on whether you are a piste skier or a climber, this is either an extremely strenuous way of obtaining a downhill run, or a soft option for aging alpinists. I am very much a climber on planks, my usual stance is a despairing snowplough and I do not feel safe unless my skis are at least a foot apart. But I am not yet aging and I am puritan enough to regard drugs as even less desirable artificial aids than expansion bolts. I miss the long full days of the summer. Though neither the skiing nor the climbing would be difficult, Dick's plan offered a tour that would be as physically demanding as a summer route, with the added incentive of covering ground in a way never possible when climbing. To cross six passes and ski seventy kilometres of glaciated country in a day would be mountain travel with a vengeance.

In the event, we did not emerge from the hut to a cold, clear night till 12.30. We cramponed down the steep moraine bank west of the hut, then skied cautiously to the foot of the rognon where the long climb up the Zmutt glacier begins. Conditions were icy and harscheisen (ski crampons) essential. Really, proper crampons would have been more suitable: harscheisen are invaluable on crust or névé but less effective on ice. Halfway up a steep slope one of mine bent 90° sideways, causing a retaining clip on the ski to shear under the strain.

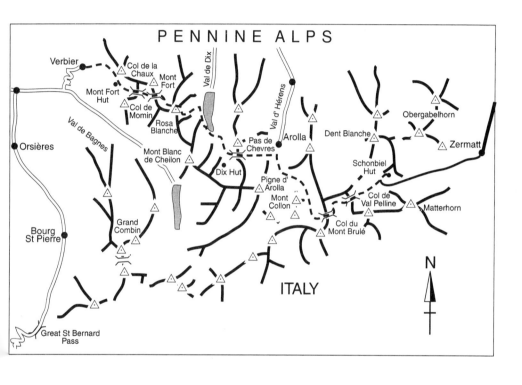

PENNINE ALPS

Verbier

Col de la Chaux

Mont Fort

Mont Fort Hut

Col de Momin

Rosa Blanche

Val de Dix

Val d' Hérens

Orsières

Val de Bagnes

Mont Blanc de Cheilon

Pas de Chevres

Arolla

Dent Blanche

Obergabelhorn

Zermatt

Schonbiel Hut

Dix Hut

Pigne d' Arolla

Mont Collon

Col de Val Pelline

Matterhorn

Bourg St Pierre

Grand Combin

Col du Mont Brulé

ITALY

N

Great St Bernard Pass

49

Fortunately the snow became softer soon afterwards and we did not meet anything seriously icy again. Now it was just a matter of following an intricately entwined mass of descending ski tracks, all of which converged whenever a crevasse became apparent, so route-finding was no problem

Torch batteries came and went, and by 4.15am we were on top of the Col de Valpelline. We had overestimated the time required and as a result it was still pitch dark. Instead of the pleasant run down to the foot of the Col du Mont Brulé we had been looking forward to, we descended in a series of careful traverses, skins still on the skis. It was light, however, by the time we reached the top of the col, and as we took the skins off with numb, clumsy fingers prior to side-slipping down the couloir on the far side, a fiery glow was creeping along the jagged skyline to the east. The sky, still deep indigo overhead, was cloudless. It promised to be a perfect day.

A wind had been tidying up the Arolla glacier and the Haute Route trail to the Col de l'Evêque was barely discernible. As yet, we had the mountains to ourselves. When we parted from the old track and headed down the glacier in a long, gentle, quietly hissing glide, it was with a sense of mingled power and privilege similar to that with which an artist, filled with a creative idea, must approach a clean canvas or a block of marble. Alas, the runes I carved upon that unsullied surface would have delighted no connoisseur. But there was no-one to see, the young sleep-flushed world was all our own, and we wheeled our way down the glacier in a glorious orgy of unmeaningful self-expression.

Ribbons of snow transported us along the valley floor to within a mile of Arolla, and just after 7am we entered the palatial Hotel Mont Collon in search of a pre-arranged breakfast. As we were escorted past immaculately coiffeured skiers down a long corridor to the dining room, I hastily plucked lumps of ice from my beard and tried to look respectable. Unfortunately, the ice started melting in my hand, leaving a trail of drips down the corridor. Panicking, I furtively dropped it behind a door for some luckless chambermaid to discover. The dining room exuded an aura of Edwardian elegance. Its highly polished wooden floor gleamed, walls and ceiling were beautifully panelled, and carved wooden pillars did their best to split up its dauntingly empty expanse into segments. There were two waiters with little to do but attend to our needs. The first fitted his surroundings perfectly, tall and aloof, with a little moustache. He brought us a basket containing four slices of bread and a pat of butter and a pot of jam each. The second waiter, short and plump, slightly spotty and with long lank hair, was less of a period piece. He took one look and brought us a whole plateful of butter and jam and not only more bread but rolls and croissants also. Steadily the mound of butter wrappers and jam pots in the middle of the table rose until it threatened to overtop the coffee pot. Our eating, once the first pangs had been satisfied, was methodical and conscientious. Residents, sauntering in for breakfast, hastily averted their eyes and made for the other side of the room.

At last capacity was reached and we walked, rather heavily, to the ski tow a hundred yards away. Enquiry over the phone had revealed that this was the penultimate day on which it would be running. A glance at the snowless slopes made one doubt whether it had, in fact, been running for weeks. More as a formality than with any real hope, we approached the deserted shack at the bottom. Suddenly to our surprise, a door opened and a head looked out. Yes, the lift *was* working. When would it start? Whenever we liked. This carefree attitude apparently did not extend to free tickets and Dick had learnt by bitter experience in the past that an instructor's licence broke no ice here. Different tactics were needed. "Je suis le guide," he announced importantly, adding, with an apologetic glance in my direction, "Il est le client." I attempted to look suitably wealthy although I suspect that the patches on my breeks would have given the game away if nothing else did. The lift attendant merely snorted, however, and let us through on the one ticket.

Having walked 100 metres up the hillside to find a tenuous thread of snow beneath the wires, we were whisked up 400 metres at breakneck speed. I am convinced that the attendant maliciously turned the engine on to full power for our benefit. Hurtling like an unskilled rodeo rider over a series of switchback bumps, scraping noisily over patches of soil and grass, and frantically lifting first one ski and then the other to avoid wickedly protruding boulders I somehow made it to the top.

We found ourselves in a beautiful hanging valley leading up to the Pas de Chèvres. The route is unglaciated and straightforward, leaving one free to enjoy a fine view of the Pigne d'Arolla, an impressively steep mountain from this side, though it is often traversed from east to west on skis. From the col, metal ladders take one down 30 metres of vertical rock to easier ground. I should imagine that even 'les chèvres' found the pass a problem before the ladders were erected. While we waited for two Italians who were on their way up the ladders, we switched on our Autophons. These are little RT devices with a range of 60 metres which increasing numbers of ski tourers carry in order that they can locate each other in the event of an avalanche. Speed is of the essence if an avalanche victim is to be dug out alive.

On the far side of the Glacier de Cheilon we could see the Cabane des Dix, the great triangular face of Mont Blanc de Cheilon looming over it, but we headed north, straight down the glacier, until forced over to the west bank by the gorge running into the Lac des Dix. The skiing was all that Spring skiing should be, on a frozen surface just beginning to thaw. Even I could turn on it, in a faltering zigzag, and Dick swooped down in a series of graceful arcs. The previous month, we learnt later, a guide going ahead to assess the danger of the steep slope that descends to the lake, had been carried away by a slab avalanche. But there was little fear of avalanche now — in places we were side-stepping down grass.

The route along the west shores of the lake is another notorious avalanche trap, usually regarded as risky until May. It was now April 19th. But even high up on the threatening east slopes there was relatively little snow and it was not yet midday, so we had no qualms about continuing. Langlauf — heels up but without skins — proved the quickest way of travelling along the undulating track beside the lake, and before long we were starting up the 900 metre haul to the Rosablanche (3336 metres). There is another route to the south which involves slightly less climbing, but we calculated that going over the summit of the mountain would be both safer and, in the long run, quicker, as well as giving a magnificent viewpoint. It was a hot, tiring climb under the afternoon sun, the only relief being a delicious little stream which broke free from the snow just long enough for a drink and a quick cool splash to a sweating brow. Despite the thin snow cover, the traverse of a south and east-facing slope to reach the little Glacier de Mourti felt a definite avalanche risk, though fortunately short. The north side of the glacier itself was littered with avalanche debris. From the col at the head of the glacier, a short easy scramble carrying skis brought us, at 4pm, to the summit of the Rosablanche where some wag had planted a miniature fir tree. It was obviously a popular ski mountain, for down below a maze of tracks led away in all directions, including towards the Col de Momin, our next objective. The broad hump of Mont Blanc dominated the view to the west; not far to the south, hazily seen against the light, lay the sprawling mass of the Grand Combin, lesser peaks clustered about it like obsequious courtiers; and far away to the south-east were the unmistakable profiles of the Matterhorn and Dent d'Hérens, afternoon cloud clinging, precariously it seemed in the perfection of the day, to their tops. With a glow of pleasure I remembered watching their changing outlines against the starlit sky as we had skied beneath them that morning.

The snow on the north side of the mountain had remained a beautiful powder. Carried away, I became over-venturesome and swiftly paid the penalty. The trouble with skiing in woollen breeches and sweater is that snow clings to wool as tenaciously as any burr, and a fall transforms one into a snowman. Moreover, a really purposeful crash usually means breeches full of snow which comes in at the top and is prevented by gaiters from escaping at the bottom. After two such harrowing experiences in quick succession, I reverted to the snowplough.

The Col de Momin to the Col de la Chaux presented no problems, but only because the weather was good and we had a track to follow. This area is complex and in poor visibility, without a track, route finding could be extremely difficult. It is potentially dangerous too, though judging by the debris, most of the snow had already come down.

The approaches to the Col de la Chaux, our final col, were in shadow by now, and it was with the never-failing thrill of emerging from darkness into light that we stood on top in the warm gold of evening, taking off skins, already freezing rigid, for the last time. Down below, on a prominent knoll beside the glacier, stood the Cabane Mont Fort, for so long a goal, suddenly a tangible reality.

One and a half hours later, and nineteen hours after leaving the Schönbiel, having traversed the hillside below the hut to the ski complex known as la Ruinette, and descended the icy remnants of a piste, we were walking the last few hundred feet down towards Verbier. The sun, which had played so large a part in the pleasures and anxieties of the day, had bowed and gone, leaving the mountains sharply silhouetted against a backdrop of flawless pink. Neon signs in the town flickered, garishly like ill-chosen footlights to the show. Intent on beating the dark, we had scarcely noticed the last act of the drama. Now the curtain was dropping. We had won the race, but for a moment, I almost wished we hadn't.

# NORTH FACE DIRECT (1975)

I'm not sure how it happened. My axe had been stuck into a lump of snow, leaving both hands free for a lay-away up a protruding fin of rock. One moment I was poised on a steep slab, coated with ice too thin and snow too rotten to offer any security, contemplating an unpromising future. The next I was watching numbly as the axe, flashing in the sunlight, cartwheeled down a sheet of ice and disappeared over the rock wall at the bottom. Comprehension of what I had done slowly dawned. Incredulity gave way to shame, and shame, as so often, took refuge in anger. Dick Renshaw never said a word. He did not even *look* reproachful. So there was no one to be angry with but myself. What a place to lose an axe — halfway up the Droites, with 600 metres of steep snow and ice below and 500 metres of ice-smothered rock above. Morale sank to a nadir. There seemed no option but to retreat. I did not fancy continuing up such difficult ground or, for that matter, descending the steep snow on the far side of the mountain with only a short, wooden-handled hammer.

It was ten in the morning. If nothing else, we had plenty of time to get off the mountain. I teetered precariously down a few feet, reversed a tension traverse in a slithering, scratching swing and was lowered the rest of the pitch from a peg. Then downwards over the icefield, pitch after pitch, swapping the axe over to share the strain of being at the sharp end. Climbing down on ice is unnerving at the best of times. With a drop of that magnitude unavoidably before one's eyes, it was doubly so. At first it was genuine ice, hard and glinting; then, worse, snow which had been a joy to climb on the way up but now was just a treacherous camouflage for the ice beneath. To make matters worse, the sun, tip-toeing along the rim of the face far above, was throwing things at us. Sheets of ice peeled away from the rock every few minutes, to break into lumps as they bounced, gather up loose snow lying in their path and, with diabolic accuracy, rush straight at us. I felt like an insect in one of those public urinals that flush automatically at regular intervals. Being snow, not stones, once we had survived a few such avalanches, they were more alarming than dangerous; but once or twice the spindrift threatened to become suffocating and there was always the fear of a really big hit which would be more than just painful.

In time, the sun went and we found ourselves descending through cloud down, down, down, each to the other a vague shape materialising only to disappear again as pitch succeeded pitch. The snow steepened to almost 70° on the rib running through the slabs near the bottom. A groping traverse through the gloom, crampons scraping every now and then on rock; then once more down through snow, deep and wet, crossing the bergschrund blindly and wallowing thigh-deep in the avalanche cone. Stars appeared as we crossed the glacier, and on the moraine we met parties bound for the Couturier Couloir. We stumbled into the workmen's doss behind the new five-star hut at midnight, exactly twenty-four hours after leaving it.

* * * * *

The North Face Direct of Les Droites (to distinguish it from the Lagarde Couloir and the North East Spur, both of which have in the past been dignified by the title of North Face) from the glacier appears to be divided into three equal sections. The bottom third is composed of rock slabs which are sometimes obliterated by snow but which, by mid-summer, can be completely bare; the central third is an icefield, black and forbidding for most of the year and, like most ice slopes, best caught in early summer or in autumn; the top third is rock permanently enmeshed in ice. Although the slabs can be extremely difficult, it is this top section that provides the steepest and most technical climbing. There is no obvious line up it and probably every ascent is by a slightly different route. Moreover, the division into thirds is an illusion created by foreshortening; from the top of the Chardonnet it can be seen that the upper rocks in fact comprise more like half the face than a third. On the epic first ascent in September 1955, despite reaching the top of the icefield in one day, Phillippe Cornau and Maurice Davaille bivouacked five times on the face.

The weather broke and it was ten days before we ground a second time up the stony piste from Argentière. Securely attached to my person with wristloop and cord was a shiny new Chouinard axe. This time we found a comfortable ready-made gîte on rocks below the Grands Montets. Not that it would have mattered where we spent the night. As usual before a big route, I scarcely slept a wink and Dick seemed almost as restless.

At midnight we were up and away, scrunching beneath the Verte, only occasionally falling through the crust. The moon was out of sight, but across the glacier it had fashioned a big white prick-eared owl which lay on one wing across the Chardonnet surveying us. Snow conditions on the face were even better than before. We did not need the rope until the snow ribbon finally ran into bare ice, a mere three rope-lengths below the slender spur which hangs down from the upper rocks. As day spread across the sky, we breakfasted at the foot of the spur, watching little dots moving just perceptibly up and down the south side of the Argentière.

In the valley we had looked more closely at the French guide. Instead of attempting to go straight up the middle of the face where the ice was only the thinnest of veneers over almost crackless slabs, this time we followed the left edge of the spur on steepening ice until a series of grooves and chimneys slanted rightwards towards its crest. The climbing was difficult but, when flakes and cracks had been cleared of snow, surprisingly well-protected. It was here that we came across two pegs, the only ones we found on the route. All was not well with the weather, however. A sinister band of iron grey in the west had been insidiously expanding, growing ever larger and blacker. There could be no doubt that real weather was on the way, not just an afternoon shower.

On the other hand, we were halfway up the face and our previous experience did nothing to make retreat an attractive proposition. We decided to 'wait and see' which, in effect, meant climbing on until the storm broke. It did so even sooner than we had expected, suddenly covering the sky in one swift leap. As Dick bridged, jammed and mantelshelfed up the second pitch of mixed climbing, the snow began to fall. By the time I reached the footholds that comprised his stance, the wind had risen and snow was sliding off the face in torrents.

Hastily we dug out overtrousers only to discover that, despite new-fangled knee-length zips, they were not wide enough to be put on over crampons. Cursing the makers and balancing on one leg like inebriated storks, we struggled first with crampons, then with the trousers, while woollen breeches became furrily matted with snow, storing up prickly dampness for the future. By now the storm was so violent that there was no question of going either up or down. We pulled the bivi sack over our heads and, for want of anything better to do, brewed up, gingerly holding the recalcitrant petrol stove between us like an unexploded bomb. Round and over the sack and, where there was a gap between us, under it also, snow flowed almost continuously. Dick hung resignedly from the belay in his Whillans harness. Lacking such a refinement, and tied on around the waist, I found a ledge wide enough to support one cheek and waged a losing battle with the snow that sought to push me off. Occasionally there was a rumble of thunder. But it was the wind that caused most concern, seizing the nylon and shaking it in gusts that had us eyeing the stitching anxiously. Inside the sack, body heat alone kept us relatively warm; but without it, we were very much aware, no amount of down clothing would have sufficed.

In a lull six hours later, we emerged stiffly from our pink fantasy world to the grey gloom of reality and abseiled five rope-lengths down to the foot of the spur. As night fell we hacked out a platform large enough to curl up like twin foetuses and soon, despite wind and snow, we were asleep.

Towards dawn I become aware that all was still. I was not prepared, however, for the perfection of the day that greeted me when I peered through a ventilation hole. I had expected to look out on swirling mist. Instead, the only cloud to be seen was hugging the valley floor in friendly fashion. From the northern peaks of the Aiguilles Rouges in the west right round to where the bulging forehead of the North East Spur hid Mont Dolent, the horizon glowed with anticipation and as we lit the stove, the sun burst upon us. Nor was there any need to be worried about snow conditions: the face was as clean as if it had been swept by a broom.

We started to climb again, slow and hesitant at first, the ice seeming somehow steeper and harder. Nevertheless, by eleven we were back at our high point, having lost exactly a day, and Dick shuffled off rightwards along a toe ledge crossing an otherwise holdless wall. It would be tedious to describe the day's climbing in detail, but it was ice or iced-up rock all the way, hard water ice never less than 60°, frequently steeper. At times it would have warranted Scottish grade IV, usually it was more like III; not technically desperate but sustained, the strain on calves and nerves never easing. After those initial pitches on the spur, we trended left towards the middle of the face, but rarely in a straight line, more often in tortuous zigzags dictated by the thickness of the ice. Not until the blue haze of evening was filling the valleys did we emerge onto a snowfield; and a mere 60 metres higher we were once more engulfed by rock and ice.

Still well below the summit we bivouacked again, forced to make do with two separate lumps of rock, a one metre gap between us. To be covered by the bivi sack I had to sit sideways, my feet dangling in the gap, my back aching for something to lean against. Dick was better off until, in the middle of the night, half his ledge collapsed. Passing from an uneasy doze into a waking nightmare, I found him thrashing about in the bottom of the sack like a monstrous fish in a landing net.

Day came at last. It was another perfect morning, as if the mountains, having expressed their disapproval, had decided to accept our continued presence with a good grace. Once again, a string of little black dots was discernible on the Argentière. There had been none yesterday. Suddenly I felt a sense of proprietorship, born of living on and with the mountain. The people on the other side of the glacier would be back at the hut by midday, having enjoyed their climb and savoured the pure air of the heights. But they would not have been absorbed into the mountain, they would not be a part of it as we were at that moment.

Petrol fumes and frozen-fingered fumbling with the chaos of gear hanging from one ice-screw quickly brought me down to earth. Climbing again, we traversed to the right at first, then straight up on steep flaky rock which was a pleasant escape from the ubiquitous ice, until the sun reached it when, almost instantaneously, the flakes became loose in their sockets. After two pitches we were presented with a choice. Somewhere to the left lay the summit; but near at hand on the right was a tempting snow couloir descending from the Brèche des Droites. For the first time the line of least resistance and the correct line were not one and the same thing. We chose the line of least resistance. Our concern now was simply to reach the top and to descend the south-facing slopes on the other side as early in the day as possible. Eagerly we kicked up the gully until Mont Blanc and the Grandes Jorasses lay before us. Panting with heat and thirst I leant against a boulder, suddenly weak, while Dick struggled up broken rocks buried under loose snow. Then a real ridge, a sharp snow crest with axe one side, feet the other. Up and down, going strongly again, and Dick taking photos. One rope-length, two, three, horizontal distance, not vertical, but further to the summit than we had realised. Finally moving together up a last little rise, wearily, till only sky was above and far away lay the Oberland and nearer at hand were the familiar profiles of the Valais.

Sprawled on a rock we made a drink and gazed round. Two yellow butterflies came dancing by. What accident, or audacity, had brought them here? What would become of them? The parallel was too obvious. Empathy with the mountain dissolved like ground-mist under a morning sun. We were impudent intruders, vulnerable and at risk, perched upon the back of an irascible monster. And every minute the deep snow of the southern slopes was growing softer and soggier. Gathering up the rope, we began the long descent to Chamonix.

# GRANDS CHARMOZ IN WINTER (1976)

It was pelting with rain when we arrived late one night at the end of December. Chamonix, next morning, looked more like Fort William in July than one of Europe's fashionable ski-resorts. Gloomily, we splashed through the puddles in double boots, regretting the waterproofs we had left at home. We had only a week and it seemed that the most we could hope for was some piste skiing. Then, magically, the clouds cleared revealing the hard blue skies and dazzling white mountains of the postcards. We gave the snow two days' grace and set off along the smothered railway line for Montenvers, grateful for an existing trail of knee-deep craters.

We were making for the North Face of the Grands Charmoz. The Mont Blanc routes had seemed too long and too high to attempt in deep snow without acclimatisation. The Argentière basin had already received a lot of attention, and the combination of a downhill approach and a hut to stay in seemed almost like cheating. The Jorasses would have been too ambitious for us. So that left, to all intents and purposes, the Aiguilles, and in the Aiguilles I had an ambition to fulfil. Exactly 2 years before I had sat on the moraine beneath the Dru, gazing across the Mer de Glace at a face I had somehow never noticed before. Pondering its formidable yet elegant appearance — a central ice-field enclosed by rock walls above and below, and flanked by steep pinnacled ridges tapering to a spire — the Charmoz had tempted me even then as a winter climb. Being mixed it would certainly be harder than in summer, without requiring quite the same degree of masochism as a pure rock climb. And, more important, the stones for which the face is notorious would be stilled. The other three — Geoff Cohen, Henry Day and Alec Stalker — had needed little persuading that this was a suitable objective for a lightning visit to the Alps.

At Montenvers the tracks ended and we were on our own. A bitter wind was picking up the snow and playing with it. The sky, starlit and frosty when we left the valley, was filling with ominous black clouds. A solitary ptarmigan swept away down the wind. Descending steep snow we joined the line of the summer path, often indistinguishable from the white hillside, and followed it as far as the ladders — or where the ladders ought to have been. Continuing to traverse, steeply at times, rock or frozen turf not far below the surface, we came to an easy gully which led down the moraine wall to the glacier. We followed the glacier edge for half a mile till, beneath the dramatic finger of the République, we could climb without difficulty towards the little Thendia glacier. We had debated the pros and cons of snow-shoes long and anxiously before deciding against them. We were relieved, therefore, to find the snow rarely more than calf deep and, in sizeable patches, covered by a hard wind crust. The weather was not so promising, though. Angry clouds were spilling down the Verte and the wind was gusting viciously. As we emerged from the shelter of some rocks on to the open slopes beneath the face, we were greeted by a stinging blast of drift that stopped us in our tracks. A bivouac in the snow was going to be uncomfortable. Necessity is the mother of invention, however, and casting around for alternatives, my eye was caught by the glacier snout not far above. Beneath its left-hand end was a large cavity. What better place for a bivouac, provided the glacier did not choose to lurch forward. Geoff and I climbed up to it and set to work filling in holes between fallen blocks, chopping away ice and shovelling snow — thankful, not for the last time, that we had brought a shovel. By the time the snow-encrusted forms of Alec and Henry appeared out of the mobile murk, a palatial platform, large enough for four and completely sheltered, was waiting to be occupied. We settled down for the night snugly but with little hope for the climb.

When I next looked at my watch, I could hardly believe it. It was 6 o'clock. I had slept for 12 hours. Geoff heaved himself upright to look out of the cave. "Look," he exclaimed, "stars!" Startled out of sleep we sat up and hastily began brewing. An old Gaz cylinder did not make for speed, however, and it was 8 o'clock before we were moving and another hour before we roped up at the foot of a steep snow-filled corner.

In the north were some little fishy clouds, but they swam away and nothing bigger came to chase them. Across the glacier the Dru, snow-free and sunlit, looked inviting. Not so the rock above us; Grade IV in summer, it was considerably more difficult now. There was surprisingly little ice in the cracks but unconsolidated snow everywhere. It was a matter of rock-climbing in crampons, and trusting untrustworthy snow. After a few feet I realised that I would have to leave my sack behind.

While Henry and Alec jumared up, we emerged on to snow, turning a rock buttress on the left before making a long traversing movement right, crampons grating on rock from time to time, probing for a weakness in the walls above. Finally, a short chimney, where again I had to sack-haul, and a ramp leading yet further right, gave access to a small snow-field between rockbands. With alarm we realised it was already 4 o'clock, only an hour till dark. Moving together up soft but stable snow, we set off diagonally leftwards, at last gaining height. Henry and Alec arrived at the chimney some time later. Deciding that they were climbing too slowly, they retreated. We did not see them again, but they reached the cave that night and descended to Chamonix without incident the following day.

Meanwhile, Geoff and I reached the upper rim of the snow-field. Geoff belayed to a Deadman — another piece of equipment we were glad to have brought — while I tip-toed up some slabs which were covered with powder but without a trace of ice or snow-ice for crampons to bite on. The Verte was glowing a lurid pink. The light of La Flégère téléphérique station, miles away across the valley, was already a brilliant green. Dark was near at hand and we were without a bivouac site. Hurriedly Geoff led through, making for a spike of rock protruding from the snow. At least it would be a belay. As night fell Geoff draped ropes and gear from the spike while I shovelled snow from unpromising bits of rock. Luckily, one of them turned out to be neither a slab nor embedded in ice. A few minutes' vigorous digging and we had a ledge which was not only flat but spacious enough to lie down on. Unfortunately its advantages were offset by the spindrift that poured down the face every few minutes, threatening us with speedy burial when we tried to ignore it.

We were slow getting away next morning. After a bivouac, not only is the body reluctant but the mind is sluggish, inhibited by the sheer number of different tasks to be performed — not to mention the nightmare of dropping a boot or a crampon. I wasted an hour on a false line, so once again it was 9 o'clock before we were properly under way, climbing ice in a shallow gully that split the rock. The top was overhanging but a hidden chimney avoided the issue and emerging, we found ourselves on the central ice-field at last. So far we had underestimated both the length and the difficulty of the route. We wondered, with some trepidation, how we would find the steep couloir at the top, which we had always expected to be hard.

In the meantime, the ice-field proved to be not ice but snow, on which we could safely move together. Gradually the snow-powdered obelisk of the République grew and became huge and the couloir began to hang overhead threateningly. In time, tired muscles reduced us to pitched climbing; but soon after we met ice where we would have used the rope in any case. Once, a small aircraft shot from behind the north west ridge in a sudden rush of noise. Without noticing us, it flew on up the glacier and back past the Dru, a cheerful speck of red in the white landscape. The ice-field was being funnelled between rock walls now. The ice became harder and steeper. Finally we were gazing with alarm at a near-vertical wall of flakes and boulders embedded in a matrix of ice.

The camera had just run out of film which was a pity for the climbing was spectacular; but we would not have taken many pictures. After 2 rope-lengths, night was upon us again and the camera could not have recorded the scenes that followed: the blue flame of the Gaz stove illuminating a few inches of rock in a universe of darkness as I stood brewing up on a tiny stance, Geoff crouched in a sleepy huddle at my feet; the faint torch blur moving to and fro far above when we climbed on; the dim shape below, from which issued frenzied strains of 'The Balls of O'Leary' as Geoff 'did his Devil's Dance on each microscopic stance'; moonlight glimmering on the far side of the couloir while, too tired to face the ice when it reappeared, we groped endlessly in chimneys and grooves and the cold nibbled like barracuda at extremities; or the moment when I emerged into the moonlight on the crest of the NE ridge, a dream of folded, twisted white writhing into the dark, and in a state of trance gazed round from the silhouetted finger of the Géant, over the deep trough of the Leschaux glacier and the delicate pale fan of the Talèfre, to the familiar yet glisteningly strange forms of the Courtes, Droites and Vertes, and on to the long glow-worm of the Chamonix valley. It was almost 3 o'clock before we bivouacked, just below the summit.

The last few feet, the following morning, seemed as hard as anything on the climb. First a deceitful wall, far steeper than it looked, on which always the next move was clearly impossible until half-hearted digging unexpectedly revealed the crucial hold; then a vicious little corner which Geoff climbed without his sack; finally, a powder-covered slab demanding concentration right to the end. Perched uneasily on the top without a belay, I brought Geoff up, conscious more of thirst than of triumph. For myself, the cold had never been a serious problem, except when I took my gloves off to climb; but a dry mouth and an unsatisfied longing for liquid had been with me almost from the start.

Alpine summits are rarely places for contemplation, let alone congratulations; there is always the descent to worry about. Despite the view of Mont Blanc and the Aiguilles and, near at hand, the amazing ice-tipped lance of the Grépon, this one passed almost unnoticed in a grovelling, burrowing but nevertheless fruitless search for an abseil spike. Eventually we left one of the four remaining pegs, reluctantly for we expected to need them all lower down. In the event, however, the six abseils down the Charmoz-Grépon couloir were all from good flakes and blissfully uneventful. On the Nantillons glacier the crevasses were choked, the séracs silent. In Leslie Stephen's words, the pulse of the mountains was beating low. After a pause on top of the rognon, we eschewed the rocks of the usual descent and passed rapidly down the middle of the glacier. Soon we were safely out of sérac range on a snow-ridge which in summer would have been a lateral moraine.

With the relief of jousting knights emerging from their armour, we threw off rucksacks, hammers, helmets, crampons, ropes, slings, anoraks and mittens and stretched out luxuriously in the last few minutes of mellow sunlight. Ski tracks led away towards Plan de l'Aiguille, contouring round hollows and hummocks beneath the Blaitière. Unbeknown to us, some of them had been made by Alec and Henry, come to look for us only a few hours earlier. The tracks would not make the going any easier but they saved us the mental effort of picking a route.

As we trudged homeward, ploughing a dark furrow across shadowy snows, the day was dying. Across the Chamonix valley the tips of the Aiguilles Rouges were alight. High above the Nantillons, the ramparts of the Charmoz and the Grépon glowed the fiercer as shadow bit into them. Before us, the sky burned with an orange ever more intense. The last téléphérique from the Midi slowed and halted before Plan de l'Aiguille station, swinging silhouetted like a bird hovering before its nest. It was one of those evenings when one would like eyes in the back of the head to take it all in.

We were tired and it was hard work breaking trail. But much of it was downhill and there was no hurry — we were not going to reach Chamonix that night. Except for the occasional elephant trap between boulders, feet could be left to themselves. Gratefully, our minds returned to the summit and peered back down the North Face on to the last 4 days. Suddenly, the delicate mauve gauze of an afterglow spread out from the orange west, its fingers brushing across the sky. Behind us, above the Aiguille de l'M, the sky was deepening from blue to vibrant indigo. The whole sky throbbed with colour, resisting the imperceptible yet inevitable onset of darkness. It was, I mused, a metaphor. Our climb, too, had been a blaze of colour, a surge of energy, a metamorphosis.

In the silence, a generator buzzing on top of the Midi carried clear and incongruous across thousands of feet of cold air. Momentarily I was resentful. Then it seemed not to matter. My content, like the silence of the winter Alps, was too deep to be disturbed. Like the poet, I could but exclaim: 'World, I cannot hold thee close enough!'

# RASSEMBLEMENT (1977)

Every other year since 1957, with only occasional gaps, the French government has sponsored an international gathering of alpinists at Chamonix, under the auspices of ENSA — the Ecole Nationale de Ski et d'Alpinisme. The hospitality of these meets has become legendary. Not only are board and lodging on a sumptuous scale provided in the valley, but huts, hill food, téléphériques and any other transport are also paid for. Last summer, to our huge delight, Geoff Cohen and I were chosen by the Alpine Climbing Group to attend the 1976 Rassemblement. Our selection was thanks only to the absence in foreign parts of those better qualified but, like winners of the football pools, we did not question whether we deserved our good fortune, we just set out to enjoy it.

However, despite eager anticipation, we missed the opening of the meet. While the speeches were being made, the 'flower of British alpinism', as Geoff remarked ironically, was abseiling down (and on two occasions prusiking back up) the Peigne in pitch dark and pouring rain. Sodden, and with no bivouac gear, it seemed preferable to keep moving, despite the lack of a torch. By four in the morning we were only two or three hundred metres above Chamonix, but there the darkness in the forest became total and we lay down on the path till daybreak. More than a little sheepish, we squelched into ENSA's domed reception hall and introduced ourselves. To our surprise, nobody was in the least perturbed; and in fact, the whole meet was to be characterised by a pleasant lack of formality. Soon we were meeting André Contamine, whose climb we had been attempting on the Peigne, and who can draw topos out of his head, with details of every piton, pitch and variation, for almost any route in the Mont Blanc range; also, Henri Agresti and Raymond Renaud, the two highly experienced and widely travelled 'Professors of Alpinism' who had been appointed mentors to the Rassemblement. Upstairs, in our ninth-floor apartment, a long hot shower washed away the less pleasant memories of the night and we emerged ready to do justice to the four course meal and unlimited wine served at lunchtime.

The chief object of such a gathering is to allow climbers of different nationalities to meet, make friends, and swap views and ideas in a relaxed atmosphere. Sixteen countries were represented, mostly European, but including the USA, Japan, India and Greece. Surprising absentees were the Italians, Austrians and Russians. A few people had met before: Raymond Renaud and Lhatoo Dorjee, for instance, had been together on the Franco-Indian expedition to Nanda Devi; and I had briefly encountered Henri Agresti in Teheran, eight years before, when we were both outward bound for the Hindu Kush. Mostly, however, it was a case of having mutual friends and acquaintances. Squadron Leader Battacharya from India had been Liaison Officer to the Army expedition to Menthosa. Marian Piekatowski had climbed with Paul Nunn on the Dru. Ulrich Eberhardt, from Munich, had been a guest of the BMC the previous Spring and spoke with some awe of the drinking as well as the climbing abilities of the National Officer, Pete Boardman. Dominique Marchal knew the climbs of the Llanberis Pass as well as we did, and the complexities of its social life considerably better. Conversation at meal-times was a lively confusion of broken French and English as Greeks talked to Spaniards, Poles to Indians, Yugoslavs to Norwegians, and Finns to Japanese.

Nevertheless, despite interesting company, lavish cuisine and a fine library to browse in, time began to drag as the weather remained bad. After a climb, the first day of idleness is always bliss, the second OK, the third is boring, the fourth sheer hell. Fortunately, the forecast on the fifth day was slightly more optimistic, and we departed for the Brenva face. We were both fairly fit, so we had no qualms about a Mont Blanc route, and the Brenva climbs were likely to be less affected than most by a week's fresh snow. As temperatures were exceptionally cold, we were prepared to risk the long sérac-threatened traverse to the Pear Buttress, a route much less frequently climbed than the others in Graham Brown's famous Tryptich (Sentinelle Rouge and Route Major).

In the Midi téléphérique station, Geoff broke a crampon strap. It seemed an ill-omen, but he tied the crampon on with a prussik loop, which, slightly to our surprise, proved quite adequate. The Chamonix valley had been filled with cloud but Italy was in sunshine and we congratulated ourselves on our acumen — or luck. For once, the surface of the Vallée Blanche was unsullied. There was not a track, or a pee stain, or a beer bottle to be seen and we made our way across to the Trident (Ghiglione) hut in a solitude and stillness which can usually be found only in winter. The hut too was deserted — even the guardian had tired of waiting for custom — so there was no argument over whether or not we should pay thirteen francs for a stay of four hours.

The Pear is not as natural a line as the Route Major, but it gave us an excellent climb, enhanced by there being, apparently, not another soul on the south side of Mont Blanc. The traverse, on bare rubble at first, then ice (a common combination everywhere after an unusually dry winter) was at an easy angle, and we were on the rocks well before the sun touched the séracs up above. The Pear Buttress itself was snowed up and gave enjoyable mixed climbing; and we were relieved to find that the dripping, riven prow of ice beneath which one must briefly pass at the top of the buttress, would have missed us by a few feet even if it had chosen to break off. Above, we unwisely took another, smaller buttress direct, but a good lead by Geoff extricated us from an apparent cul-de-sac. (A few days later some Swiss friends from the Meet made the mistake of following our footsteps and, lacking Geoff's expertise, they had to retreat. The moral is obvious!) The upper band of séracs is less dangerous than those below, but we seemed to be beneath them for a long time, and regretted not taking the steeper but safer line to the top of the Peuteret Ridge. We broke no records for the long slog through soft snow to the summit of Mont Blanc, and a nose-numbing wind sped us on our way down the other side without pause. We were equipped with tickets for trains, téléphériques and buses, but arrived just too late for each in turn. Discovering the hard way that my new boots were a size too small, I enjoyed the 12,000 ft descent to Chamonix less than I might have done. But even blackened toes could not wholly eradicate the sensations of a day alone with the sun and the wind on that huge face.

The following evening saw us back at the Aiguille du Midi, staying at the privately-owned Refuge des Cosmiques, in order to try the Gervasutti Pillar on Mont Blanc du Tacul. No longer regarded as difficult, it is still a magnificent climb, especially in its central section where it goes straight up the crest of a startlingly slender pillar of perfect yellow granite. The forecast had been for good weather in the morning, deteriorating in the afternoon. Since the hardest climbing is in the bottom half, that seemed fair enough. In the event, the sun was obscured by high cloud almost as soon as it appeared over the horizon, and a North wind forced us to wear windproofs and fingerless mitts from the word go. We seemed to be shivering all day. There was so much snow still lying, thanks to the low temperatures, that crampons became necessary half way up, just after the last graded pitch. About noon, the weather broke as predicted, and with driving snow and wind gusting from every direction, it all felt very Scottish. Easy climbing became difficult, sometimes desperate, and the upper ridge seemed to go on for ever. We were still climbing as dark fell, and the final pitch stretched to 250 ft as, unbeknownst to each other, we moved together across a steep mixed wall which, even in the depths of night created by my dark glasses, felt exposed. On top the snow had stopped but it was still blowing and we could see nothing, so we dug a platform out of a snow arête, and pulled the Zdarsky sack over our heads. I had a lightweight sleeping bag and a small square of Karrimat, and was very snug. Geoff, who had a duvet and only the ropes for insulation, did not fare so well and, next morning, was noticeably more anxious to be on the move. Though we knew the descent, travelling among crevasses in poor visibility is never pleasant and we were glad when, halfway down the steep north slope of the Tacul, we suddenly dropped out of the cloud. Soon we were back at the Cosmiques, having breakfast and trying to make friends with its anglophobe guardian.

A day of rest was called for after this excursion and, at a hint from Henri who had chanced to see my crampons one day, we took the opportunity to visit the Charlet-Moser equipment works. M. Charlet was affable and generous. After a glass of cognac, we came away clutching not only a pair of fourteen-point crampons apiece but also a Gaberou axe and a North Wall hammer respectively. Such fine new gear deserved a worthy baptism so, fortified by a good forecast and able to be extravagant at someone else's expense, we took the cable car up to the Grands Montets and bivouacked at the edge of the chaotic Nant Blanc glacier.

Next day, in twelve exhilarating hours, we made a new climb on the Nant Blanc face of the Aiguille Sans Nom, a shoulder of the Aiguille Verte. Taking the buttress between the traditional Charlet-Platonov route and the more recent Boivin-Vallencant, at the bottom it was easier but also much safer than either. The central ice-field, covered by an inch or so of snow-ice, presented no problems. And in the upper rocks we zigzagged up a thin but continuous ribbon of ice which gave climbing similar to that on the North Face of Les Droites, less sustained, but technically rather harder.

The climbing was enjoyable throughout, the discovery of a way through the rock-band, exciting. Our Charlet gear proved excellent and we climbed with confidence. But the best was yet to come. Beneath us, as we traversed the delicate Sans Nom ridge to the summit of the Verte, the valleys were filled with cloud, rising, falling, boiling, swirling, no mere cotton-wool carpet but as mobile and ever-changing as the sea. We took our time, pausing to gaze around, lingering on the top. Why hurry down to a stuffy, overcrowded hut on such an evening? We bivouacked comfortably halfway down the Grand Rocheuse with a wide-angled view from the deepening sunset hues of Mont Blanc across to the Jorasses, jutting out of the cloud like a rock above a foaming sea of ruddy gold, and on to

67

the dissolving blues, greys, purples and violets in the east over the Triolet. The sun was finally fading from the tops and we were settling into our sleeping bags when suddenly the shadow of the Verte appeared on the cloud below us, an enormous cone appearing to stretch all the way to the Pennine Alps. As the stars came out and night crept over us, we lay silent and wide-awake on our respective ledges, reluctant to let the day pass into memory.

Back in the valley, the weather broke and climbing was out of the question for some time. After the activity of the last few days, we welcomed the chance to relax and see how the others had been faring. In the past, a feature of the Rassemblement has been fierce competition between leading climbers, fostered rather than discouraged by the organisers, and the wags did not fail to dub this year's meet the Climbing Olympics. To our relief, however, competition this time was minimal and never overt. Climbs were recorded but not publicised. Good routes were being done but, perhaps because of the unsettled weather, nothing exceptional. Our attitude towards the Rassemblement and, I suspect, that of most of the other participants, was simply that here was a once-in-a-lifetime opportunity to climb free of all financial considerations and we wanted to make the most of it. It is also easier to climb intensively when you are living on a good diet, with a drying room, hot shower and comfortable bed to return to, rather than lurking in a tent somewhere in the forest.

At all events, when Henri Agresti suggested that we join him, his wife Isabelle, and Bernard Muller in an attempt on the Pilastro Rosso — the Red, or Left-hand Pillar of Brouillard — we were initially delighted, and it was concern at the size of the party rather than rivalry that caused us to opt for the Right-hand pillar instead. Seen from the valley, the Brouillard pillars appear insignificant outcrops perched high on the south flank of Mont Blanc. Close to, they are superb granite monoliths that would delight the eye of any rock climber. Both give something like 1500 ft of mostly free climbing in an extremely remote setting from which retreat, if not quite as difficult as from the neighbouring Frêney Pillars, is nonetheless uninviting. The Left-hand Pillar, first climbed by Walter Bonatti, exits directly onto the long and rarely-climbed Brouillard ridge, but from the top of the Right-hand Pillar there is a further 1500 ft of mixed climbing to reach the ridge. Not quite so fine a line as Bonatti's route, the Right-hand Pillar has had even fewer ascents since it was first climbed, at the third attempt, by a British/American team in 1965. Bonington and Harlin, the leading rope, turned back well below the Brouillard ridge, and it is possible that in the intervening ten years the route had never been completed to the summit of Mont Blanc.

Time was running out now, so at the first hint of a good forecast all five of us drove through the Tunnel and started the 7000 ft walk up out of the Val Veni. We were late away and it was under an afternoon sun that we toiled up steep snow slopes towards the Eccles bivouac hut. The snow was deep and wet, and while we rested on a small rock island, with an innocuous hiss the entire slope we had just crossed slid away from the ice beneath, wiping out our tracks. Sobered, we sat on our rock listening to Geoff reading aloud from W H Murray's Mountaineering in Scotland, until the sun disappeared and the temperature dropped. We reached the hut as night fell. The Eccles hut is a tin chicken coop lashed with wire onto the crest of a buttress overlooking the Brouillard glacier. Equipped with four bunks, its accommodation is hardly palatial even for two. We arrived to find it already occupied. The residents, two Japanese bound for the Central Pillar of Frêney and two English for the Innominata Ridge, were in bed and less than pleased to see us ...

Next morning found the five of us on the Right-hand Pillar. Henri and party had discovered that to reach their pillar would have involved an irreversible abseil over a bergschrund and they preferred to have a line of retreat. Progress was slow, being hindered by snow in corners and chimneys, the dropping of the guidebook, and some unskilful aid climbing. The route described in both English and French guides, and which we followed, more or less, is curiously unsatisfying in its lower half, seeming to avoid the issue by sidling off to the right of the pillar. In retrospect, the huge corner in the centre, taken by Bonington and Rusty Baillie on their first two attempts, would give both better climbing and a better line. However, the weather was perfect, the situation magnificent, the company of the French entertaining. And, once into the middle of the upper pillar, the climbing was superb. As we neared the top, the sun sank and the sky darkened. Searching for a bivouac site, we climbed on. The last pitch of 5 sup. was a blind, clutching swing from an unseen peg, landing us on an ice-arête that had to serve for the night.

Next day the sky was veiled with cirrus. We ran out the rope eleven times up a broad snowy spur before reaching the Brouillard ridge, encountering serious mixed climbing when we turned a rock tower on the left and found, to our surprise, that the spur narrowed near the top to a precarious knife-edge of snow. The cloud was dropping and the wind rising as we hurried along the loose and delicate Brouillard ridge to Mont Blanc de Courmayeur, on to the summit — always further than expected — and down to the Goûter hut. The Agrestis and Bernard, a couple of hours behind, fought their way over in a full-scale blizzard and counted themselves lucky to find the Vallot refuge on the descent. We all met up again the following morning and, in company with the two or three hundred people who had been foiled in their attempt on Mont Blanc by the Goûter route, returned to Chamonix.

The Rassemblement ended the same evening at a buffet banquet attended by Maurice Herzog and the Mayor of Chamonix. Two enormous salmon formed a centrepiece and Beaujolais was by the barrel. Afterwards, thirty odd climbers adjourned to Henri and Isabelle's barn in the woods above Les Houches, to drink coffee and home-brewed wine by candlelight. The meet could not have ended on a better note.

# ALPINE GUIDE (1994)

Ian took off his pink and lilac rucksack with the rolled yellow karrimat strapped to its side, and dumped it beside the path with a grunt. His orange tee-shirt was dark with sweat and stuck to his back. I followed suit and, suddenly light-footed and free, scrambled down to the little stream that had been the excuse for a rest. I cupped my hands under a fall and drank and drank from the cold, clear water, then splashed it over my face, again and again, savouring the exquisite coolness on hot skin. Apart from a few stunted old larch trees, their limbs contorted by wind and the weight of winter snow, there is no shade on the path up to the Pelvoux refuge, not in the middle of the afternoon, anyway. Above us, the path zigzagged endlessly up a steep meadow. Little figures were dotted about it, tracking their way, some to right, some to left, laboriously upwards. The hut itself was out of sight, higher yet, reached by a hidden break in seemingly impregnable crags. All around us were flowers every bit as gaudy as ourselves — showy, orange lilies, the yellow and purple spikes of mullein, mauve and orange asters, bright pink willow-herb (the alpine variety) crimson house–leeks and many more. I pulled out the Collins Guide to Alpine Flowers from the lid of my sack and debated whether it was St. Bernard's or St. Bruno's Lily we had seen earlier. Then I lay back in the sun, arm across my eyes, and allowed body and mind to relax totally. It was a good place to be.

Much later we reached the hut. It is a solid stone–built affair, with red wooden shutters and a heli–pad in front of it. Alpine huts can be delightfully sociable places, but at the height of summer they are liable to be crowded, full of people not all of whom are making an early start in the morning. Dormitories are noisy and stuffy, sleep not easily achieved. Add to that an exceedingly grumpy guardian and his equally bad–tempered Alsatian, both of whom I had encountered already that season, and we had every incentive to bivouac. Out of sight, out of mind seemed an adage worth heeding, so we scrambled up a rock step and contoured across the hillside until we found the perfect spot, a grassy hollow studded with spring gentians and mountain pansies, not far from a stream. A hundred yards away across the stream, four chamois stood stockstill on a snowpatch watching us. Then they were off, in a four–footed glissade down the snow and away out of sight. Near at hand, young marmots were playing quite unconcerned on the slope beneath us. Suddenly there was a strident whistle. Mama had returned and was ordering her young inside in no uncertain fashion. A second later, there was not an animal to be seen.

We had a pleasant evening. Our site kept the sun till late and we lay on our mats overlooking the valley of the Celse Nière, deep in shadow, lingering over our bread and cheese and fruit. We could not emulate Whymper who, on an early ascent of the Pelvoux in 1862, had a whole cask of wine to see him through the night, and a porter to carry it. But we did have a modest plastic bottle of vin ordinaire. When the sun finally set, the earth continued to radiate warmth and it was some time before we snuggled comfortably into our sleeping bags. Even then we did not sleep but chatted desultorily, watching the planets appear and light fade from the summits. I remembered W A B Coolidge, the alpine historian and pedant, a man not given to flights of fancy, who had remarked of this same view: "One of the most striking sights ever witnessed by the present writer was from a high bivouac on the S. (sic) slope of the Pelvoux when, as daylight vanished, the eye ranged over many ridges, the crest being in each case picked out by the light, though the slope was enshrouded in darkness, these ridges fading away, little by little, towards the plains of Provence, and presenting a marvellous series of silhouettes."

Coolidge first climbed the Pelvoux in 1870 during a season in which he made the first ascents of the Ailefroide and the central summit of the Meije, the third ascent of the Ecrins, and the second ascent of the Brenva Spur on Mont Blanc. History does not relate whether his regular climbing partners, his aunt Miss Brevoort and his mongrel dog Tschingel, were present on this occasion. However, by the time he returned to the Pelvoux in 1881 and climbed the couloir that bears his name, guided by the Almers father and son, both aunt and dog were dead and he was developing the prickly sensitivity that was to earn him the soubriquet The Hedgehog of Magdalene. Today, the Coolidge Couloir is the voie normale, a popular route throughout the summer. It was our goal for the morrow.

Much of the attraction of alpine climbing lies in the likelihood that at some point the unforeseen will occur, to delight, to terrify or to confuse. We fell asleep beneath a star–filled sky but we were awakened, a few hours later, by the light patter of raindrops on our bivi–bags. Lightning flickered on the horizon. Our little nook was sheltered from the wind, but down below a loose sheet of corrugated iron on the roof of an outbuilding clattered and banged insistently. Suddenly, from nowhere, an avalanche of rocks crashed down the stream–bed a matter of yards away. I poked my head out of my sleeping bag in time to see the sparks struck as a second avalanche roared by. We were not in the line of fire, but sleep had been well and truly dispelled. Muttering, I looked at my watch. It was three o'clock, time to be moving anyway.

By the time we had breakfasted and packed our bags, lights had appeared and several parties had passed not far away with a clinking of axes and a scrunching of boots. We followed them sleepily up a slope of hard–packed moraine, to the edge of the little Clot de l'Homme glacier. It was less than fifty yards across but steep enough to warrant crampons. There was a mêlée of stooping figures and bobbing torch beams. Whymper had problems here, too. Looking back, we could see more lights approaching. The Pelvoux was going to be busy.

Beyond the glacier, moraine, steep snow and bits of slabby rock lead soon enough to the easy–angled slopes of the Sialouze glacier. By now, dawn was breaking, albeit murkily. Suddenly, with no warning at all, there was a tremendous clap of thunder. Everybody stopped in their tracks. All over the slope, little knots of climbers formed to consider the implications. Many of them turned about and descended back the way they had come. High on a peak of nearly 4000 metres is no place to be voluntarily in a thunderstorm. On the other hand, this was not only Ian's first big peak, but also the last day of his holiday. We were not inclined to give up just yet. The sky was overcast but the summit was still clear and the cloud did not appear to be dropping. There was no more thunder.

After waiting twenty minutes, we continued, pleased to note that the mountain was no longer crowded. Only one other pair followed us as we cramponed up névé away from the glacier proper onto the steeper slopes of the Coolidge couloir. Towards the top, old footprints led into an icy runnel overshadowed by crumbly–looking cliffs suggesting stonefall. We chose to move slightly left, crossing sections of block scree to link up snow patches that led eventually to the broad summit plateau of the Pelvoux. A short walk brought us to the Pointe Puiseux, 3946 metres, the higher of the two summits and, after the Ecrins and the Meije, the highest point in the Oisans.

The panorama that greeted us was dramatic, a monochrome landscape across which grey curtains of precipitation drifted menacingly. Away to the east, the mountains were inky black, distant snowfields on the Meije and the Grande Ruine standing out a livid yellowish white, like old ivory by contrast. Thunder rumbled in the distance. A rising wind whipped up the snow at our feet, but Ian's face was glowing with pleasure in the eerie, threatening light. It was a fitting culmination to his first season.

We were about to leave when the second rope arrived, a French couple whom we had met on the path the day before, cheerful, friendly people. He had last climbed the Pelvoux twenty–two years before, and their ascent obviously had sentimental significance for them both. We all shook hands, then Ian and I left the summit for them to enjoy alone. They were descending the Coolidge, so we were going to have the Violettes glacier to ourselves.

As a climb, the Coolidge Couloir is unexceptional, no more than an exercise in cramponing, it has to be said. But the complex descent down the Violettes glacier and back to Ailefroide, all 8000 ft of it, makes this one of the finest traverses in Europe. At first the glacier was straightforward but as we descended things became more exciting. There were some steeper slopes, crevasses to jump with the rope kept tight between us, a dramatic ice architecture of riven blocks and towers on either hand, and enclosing rock walls that grew higher as we lost height. Once, we had to leap ten foot down from the lip of a bergschrund: nothing unusual about that, except that a second bergschrund was yawning only feet below, waiting to snap up the clumsy or the unwary. Lower yet, we found ourselves picking a way down a rock buttress that splits the glacier. A couloir on its right flank, with a short abseil halfway down, brought us back onto the glacier at the point where it levels off briefly. Old tracks led horizontally to a brèche in the ridge beyond. It was only three hundred yards away, but threatened by huge toppling séracs and littered with avalanche debris — a place to suspend the imagination and run ...

Another short abseil and a scramble down a couloir on the far side of the brèche brought us onto a snow slope. Another rock barrier, then more snow, glissading and skating by now in slushy snow, until it ran out into ice and we took to a moraine ridge at its side. A steep dusty path wound its way down the moraine and, almost as steeply, on down a stony meadow. The sun came out with a fierce heat, though behind us the cloud had dropped, smothering the tops. We were glad to be back on terra firma. Our mouths were dry and gritty, our feet hot and sore when we reached a lovely and much–needed stream. We drank and bathed our feet and stripped down to our tee–shirts for the first time since the path up to the Pelvoux hut, twenty–four hours before. We had come full circle.

However, we were not finished yet. At the point where most paths would become progressively more amenable, this one dived abruptly downwards, following a rock rake across some extremely steep ground for several hundred feet. It was not difficult, but definitely not a place to trip, and it seemed to go on and on. The only compensation was that the vertical and overhanging rock above shielded us from the sun. It was a shock to emerge at the bottom, out of the shadow into a dry, hot world of scorched meadows and churring cicadas. The village of Ailefroide was only a few hundred metres away, but there was still a moment of excitement to come. As we picked our way through some massive fallen blocks, what should flutter away in front of us but a large, black and yellow butterfly — unmistakably a swallowtail, a beautiful creature I had last seen over ten years before in the very different setting of Wicken Fen. And so, parched and weary, we came to the little cafe on the corner as you enter the village, to sit under a parasol and drink cold beer and look back with disbelief at the way we had just come.

# Further Afield

# MOUNTAINEERING IN GRAHAMLAND (1972)

We approached Mount Charity in a spell of clear, sunny weather, after travelling through cloud on bearings for the best part of a fortnight. The southernmost of the three Eternities, it rises out of a 6000 ft plateau without noticeable glaciers or foothills to twin summits of 9000 ft. In the previous three months Malcolm McArthur and I had covered a thousand miles, sledging down the Grahamland Peninsula, through Alexander Island and across the Palmerland Plateau and, despite plans, had so far climbed nothing. Charity had been climbed at least once before and, with so many virgin peaks available, it had not been one of our original ambitions. But fine days were scarce and as we passed by on our way north, the unclimbed East Ridge of the highest summit became more and more enticing until, at last, we could resist it no longer.

Spanning the dogs high up a corrie south of the ridge, just out of sérac range, we cramponed up to a col. Above, the ridge rose as a sharp snow arête, punctuated by little outcrops of orange-brown granite, for about 1500 ft. Keeping to the snow, kicking through a layer of soft to the névé beneath, we soloed up it rapidly, feeling very fit. In a sense we had been mountaineering all summer. Negotiating crevasses, ice-falls, pressure systems or steep slopes with a sledge can be as mentally taxing as a serious climb and crossing high cols we had experienced some thrilling moments scenically. But it was a joy to be actually climbing again.

The slope steepened. Some slab echoed when I kicked it. Investigation revealed a gap between it and the underlying ice and we roped up. The sun was scorching its way through glacier cream and lip salve but my feet were numb in less than adequate footwear. Axe in one side, feet the other, and disturbing drops on both, we continued along the arête till it levelled out just before a jutting square block of a cornice. Moving on to the north side of the ridge by the simple expedient of swinging a leg over it, we traversed up and across a face, steep, icy and very exposed. Bendy old ski-mountaineering boots are not ideal for steep cramponing and we had to bear in mind our descent by the same route; so we chopped comfortable steps for three hundred feet. Then the ice became snow, the angle eased and we were there.

A cautious inspection revealed that the summit was the confined but solid apex of three corniced ridges, and we relaxed. Sitting on our sacks, drinking in the space, the silence and the sunlight, we picked out far below the two specks which were the dog teams. To the north were the massive rock walls of Mount Hope. In the west, the mountains of Alexander Island were clearly visible over a hundred miles away. Sixty miles south, we could trace the route we had taken, mostly on dead reckoning navigation, through the South Eland Mountains, a beautiful cirque of 10,000 ft peaks; and thirty miles beyond them, Mount Andrew Jackson, climbed by John Cunningham a few years ago, poked its head above the horizon. Somewhere to the east lay the Weddell Sea, but the low cloud which is the bane of the east coast had, unnoticed, obscured the view and was rising insidiously towards us. The first wisps were already eddying playfully about the base of the mountain. It was time to go.

The mist engulfed us as we sledged back to more level ground and we pitched camp in white-out. When it next lifted, two weeks later, we were far away. For we were not on a climbing holiday, we were employees of the British Antarctic Survey, and we had a job to do. Our ascent of Charity was simply a perk, made possible by a lucky conjunction of good weather and the right day.

At present BAS maintains four bases along the west coast of the Antarctic peninsula which is known as Grahamland in the north and Palmerland in the south. Argentine Island, a purely 'static' base, offers virtually no possibilities to the mountaineer. Fossil Bluff, the furthest south, is a little four-man outpost which usually confines its activities to the ice-shelf of King George VI Sound. Adelaide Island, from which the Survey's two aircraft operate in the summer, boasts half a dozen fine peaks of 4000 to 7000 ft (see the article by Bugs McKeith in the SMC Journal 1969), but for most of the year is cut off from the mainland. The fourth base, Stonington, is an unprepossessing, rocky little island, littered with debris from the two American and one British expedition that used it prior to the last twelve years of continuous occupation. Its all-important asset is a steep ice ramp, giving field parties access to the North East glacier. Once they have relayed loads up the notorious 'Sodabread Slope', ten miles further inland, they are free to sledge the length and breadth of the Peninsula. Most of the BAS geology, geo-physics and survey field programmes are based on Stonington and depend upon its twelve dog teams to cover country often too crevassed for motor vehicles. Field parties usually comprise two men, a scientist and a General Assistant, each with a team, and to sledge 2000 miles in a year is common. One of the chief qualifications for the post of GA is mountain experience, since

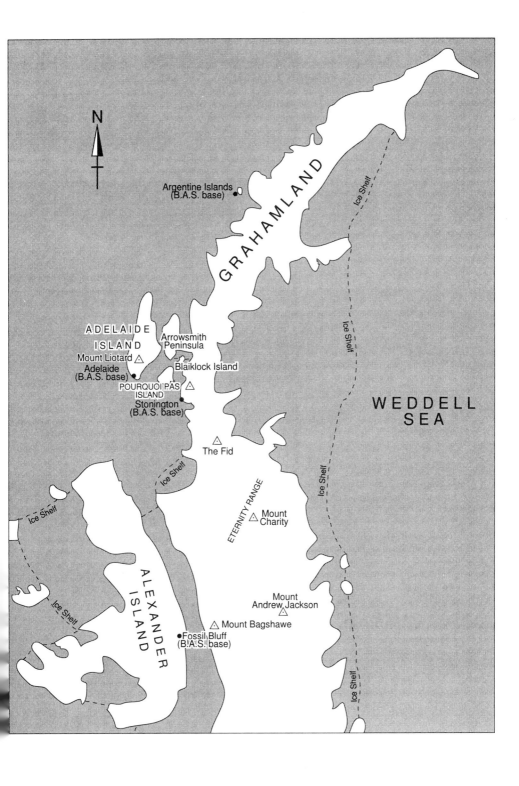

sledging in Grahamland poses many familiar, as well as some unfamiliar, mountaineering problems. It is, in many ways, akin to ski-touring. I was lucky enough to spend a year at Stonington as a GA.

It is not generally appreciated, even among climbers, that all over Antarctica there are mountains. Grahamland, in the scale and accessibility of its mountains and the beauty of its fjords, resembles a southern Greenland. Curving like a crooked finger out of the bulk of the continent, for hundreds of miles mountains and glaciers rise abruptly from its complex coastline to a 6000 ft central spine which widens into the Palmerland Plateau as the finger thickens towards its base. Travelling through intricate glacier networks, one is surrounded everywhere by unclimbed peaks — faces bigger than the Lauterbrunnen Wall, ridges comparable to the Brenva classics, spires and pinnacles reminiscent of Chamonix, and lesser peaks and rock nunataks without number. From a mountaineering point of view, Grahamland must be one of the least exploited regions left on earth. It seems a climbers' paradise. And yet the mountains remain unclimbed. True, Mount Andrew Jackson, Faith, Hope and Charity in the Eternity Range, Bagshawe in the Batterbees, Arronax on Pourquoi Pas Island, Gaudry, Leotard and Bouvier on Adelaide, these and a number of the nunataks *have* been climbed. And no doubt there have been many ascents, particularly those made to establish survey stations, that have gone unrecorded or, at any rate, unremembered. But to all intents and purposes the reservoir remains untapped.

Despite the number of competent climbers employed every year by BAS, remarkably little has been, or is being, climbed. Why? The chief reason is undoubtedly the weather, which must rival that of Patagonia. The severity of winds and temperatures, and the speed with which the weather deteriorates make caution far more necessary than in other parts of the world (though electric storms are one hazard virtually unknown). Katabatic winds of 100 mph blowing off the Plateau are by no means rare and far higher winds have been recorded. These winds can blow up from nothing in a matter of minutes; the only warning will have been a few wisps of drift at the plateau edge. And even where wind is less of a menace, weather systems are no more predictable. Temperatures lower than -30°C are unusual, even in winter, but they are quite cold enough for the slightest wind to have a drastic effect and for a bivouac to be an unpleasant prospect. All in all, one is well advised to wait for clear, settled weather before venturing onto a mountain, and such weather is infrequent. During autumn and winter it is possible to spend as much as 50 per cent of the time lying-up and, while this drops to nearer 20 per cent in the summer, one can be tent-bound for days on end at any season. Nor can sledging conditions be equated with climbing conditions. As the pyramid tent can be easily storm-pitched and a mobile home recreated within minutes of stopping, it is possible to risk travelling when climbing would be out of the question.

Only once did I try climbing in doubtful weather. That was on a peak overlooking the Reid glacier, in the Arrowsmith Peninsula, north of Stonington. At the time, we were camped beside a food depot at the very foot of the long spur which seemed the obvious way up the mountain. Gwynn Davies, the geologist with whom I was working, did not seem very interested even though he was a climber, but he was too good-natured not to come along. So one day, when visibility was too poor for plane-table mapping, rather than lie in the tent all day, we decided to give it a go. It was a fine route, a delicate notched arête of alpine length, with a blue-gouged ice-fall on one side, cicatrices sweeping up to the crest of the ridge in places, and rock walls dropping sheer to a hanging glacier on the other. But on the heavily-corniced summit ridge, visibility was nil and we found ourselves suddenly exposed to the full blast of a gale. Spectacles were soon hopelessly sheathed in ice and beards became solid lumps. Peering through the mist for the cornice edge, it was impossible to tell how far away it really was. On a wind-packed surface, crampons were leaving no imprint and it was no place to get lost on the descent. After groping our way higher and higher, skirting a sérac which loomed up in front, discovering crevasses by putting our legs through them, we eventually turned back. When we looked out of the tent in brilliant sunshine next morning, we realised to our disgust that we had been only twenty metres from the top. But it had been a salutary reminder not to underestimate the weather.

All too often, the right place and the right time do not coincide. Movements in the field are governed by the exigencies of a work programme and depot logistics. Thirty days' food for men and dogs is usually the maximum that can be carried (giving loads of about 450 kilos per sledge), and by the time scientific work has been carried out and a safe margin allowed to reach the next depot, there may be little time left for diversions. During our summer journey south, Malcolm and I sledged through two mountain groups, the Waltons and the South Elands, that had never been visited before. In each we set our sights on one particular peak that stood out both by virtue of its appearance and the ease of access to a feasible route. But either weather or fatigue thwarted us on each occasion and in neither instance did we have the food to linger.

Access can be a problem, but that is true of any glaciated mountains and it is certainly far safer to ski beside a sledge than to travel on foot. Nevertheless, the hardest part of one small peak I climbed with Gwynn, at the bottom of the Helm Glacier in the Arrowsmith, was reaching the foot of it. Leaving, as night fell and temperatures plummeted, after an easy but exhilarating day in golden autumn sunlight, my dogs suddenly chose to take a short cut, ignoring a loop in our tracks where we had skirted poorly-bridged crevasses. Before I knew what had happened, my lead bitch Morag had fallen out of her harness and was sitting, fortunately unhurt, sixty feet down a large hole. It was dark by the time I had abseiled in, attached her to a rope, jumared out and finally hauled the unfortunate dog to the surface.

Even given a fine day, remoteness renders any climb extremely serious. Travelling and working in pairs, climbers are closer to the position of Shipton and Tilman on Mount Kenya than they are to most expeditions in the Andes, the Himalaya or even Greenland. Aircraft are only available four months of the year and although sledge parties are often separated by only a day or two's travel, it could be as much as a week before failure to come up on the radio aroused serious alarm. Should a rescue operation be necessary, it would not only be costly but it might well involve international co-operation and would certainly mean the disruption of the Survey's scientific work. Moreover, it is unusual for two keen climbers to find themselves sledging together. Consequently, climbers have kept well within their limits and, to my knowledge, nothing technically difficult has been attempted. Understandably enough, BAS frown on climbing, whilst powerless to prevent it entirely. After all, you cannot employ mountaineers as such, place them in a mountain environment and expect them suddenly to lose all interest in climbing.

Finally, the nature of the climbing itself can be a deterrent. Most rock has been badly frost-shattered, making spectacular aiguilles and attractively crenellated ridges lethal to set foot upon. There are exceptions, of course. Ian Sykes has climbed a fine 600 metre pillar on Roman Four, near Stonington; and Nery Island only a mile from base, gave surprisingly enjoyable scrambling one evening. But by and large, we found rock of any description (granite is the most common) best left well alone. This was borne home to Malcolm and myself on Ridge Island. As its name implies, the island is a long thin comb of rock, 2000 ft at its highest point, rising steeply from the waters of Bourgeois Fjord. Having sledged across the fjord's winter coating of sea-ice, we had difficulty finding a strip of 'beach' wide enough to pitch the tent, and the dogs had to be spanned up a rocky slope. Six miles long, for much of its length the ridge looks closer in character to the Diable Arête than to, say, the Cuillin Main Ridge. Unfortunately, on closer acquaintance it resembles neither. We had covered less than a quarter of a mile, and had not even reached the first major gendarme, before we abandoned the route as downright dangerous. The view was superb, over grey sea-ice, broken into gigantic crazy-paving by thread-like leads of black water, to the 5000 ft walls that enclose the fjord. The positions were dramatic. But the rock, beneath an unhelpful layer of fresh powder, was simply too fragile for climbing to be in any sense enjoyable.

With so many potential obstacles, the few routes we *did* climb had all the savour of a well-earned reward. The opportunity never occurred to attempt any of the notable 'plums' such as Mount Wilcox, Bartholin Peak or The Fid. But although none of our climbs was spectacular or particularly difficult, they were unforgettable mountain days. Most memorable of all, I think, was an ascent with Malcolm of a 1200 metre peak on Blaiklock Island. Blaiklock is only an island in theory, since it is permanently attached to the Arrowsmith Peninsula by the Jones Ice Shelf. Six of us had been dropped on the Jones by ship, in March, to remain on the Arrowsmith until sea-ice enabled us to return to Stonington for mid-winter. (In the event we were not all back on base until the beginning of August.) Although sledge parties have been visiting the Jones from Stonington for years, as far as we knew only one of the myriad peaks surrounding it had been attempted, and that unsuccessfully.

We had our eyes on this particular peak for nearly two months, but it was May 15th and late in the year before weather and circumstances permitted us to climb it. However, we were far enough north for the Long Winter Night to be a myth. The sun did not finally disappear until the end of May and even at mid-winter, there remained five hours of passable daylight. So, although we harnessed the dogs by the light of a tilly lamp, the sky was tinged with saffron behind us and flushing rose in front by the time we reached Scree Cove Col, beneath the north face, an hour and a half later. It was eleven before we had picketed the dogs, exchanged canvas mukluks for leather boots and sorted out some gear, and as we plodded up the first snow slope the sun came down it to meet us, warm and friendly. The weather was perfect. Carefree and relaxed, we could consciously enjoy every minute of our day off.

Straightforward step-kicking took us up one of several couloirs seaming the rocky face. Ill-defined at first, it was etched more deeply into the mountainside as we rose, becoming steep, narrow and, in places, icy when we entered the right-hand branch of a fork. Finally it terminated in a formidable ice-cliff which was, in fact, the left wall of the summit ice-field, and curved round not far below to guard the bottom edge of the ice-field also. As I uncoiled the rope and searched for a belay, the bored, disconsolate howling of the dogs was carried to us, faint but clear, on the stillness. Behind, the huge dark mass of Rendu's 7000 ft south face still scowled down from six miles away, on the far side of the Jones Ice Shelf.

Descending a little, Malc found a weakness in the barrier, a short vertical wall. He climbed it quickly and competently, as befits one who can assess conditions on Lochnagar from his bedroom window, and disappeared over the top. There was a long pause, the sound of prolonged hammering and, at last, a slightly anxious voice asking me not to fall off. I set out hopefully brandishing a pristine Chouinard hammer, but the ice was crumbly so it had to be handholds after all. I found Malc belayed to a peg stuck optimistically into a suspicious-looking and almost vertical crack in ice which was too brittle to take a peg anywhere else. All at once, our position had become startlingly exposed. Beneath and to our left, nothing was visible between the abrupt drop of the ice-cliff and the col 2000 ft below. It looked a long way. Hastily, I embedded the pick of the Chouinard, and cut a step to stand in while I gazed at the breathtaking view down Scree Cove suddenly revealed. The richness of colouring was what gave it such impact, a long gleaming arm of black water carrying the eye straight to the gold-fired peaks of Pourquoi Pas Island, named by Charcot after his famous ship sixty years before. The ice-field itself was alight with a glow in which sunrise and sunset were inextricably merged in a single conflagration.

The ice was hard but not too steep, so we moved together to save time on a rising traverse across the face for two hundred metres of so, uncomfortably aware that a slip would mean a long, long toboggan ride for both of us, with a sizeable ski-jump en route. Meeting snow again with some relief, we headed straight up until compelled to weave our way through a number of cauliflower growths, or 'donglers', of sugary snow and rotten ice, caused by rime. The summit itself was a 'dongler', perched on top of two long ridges like the bobble on a ski-hat, giving fifty feet of steep, unstable climbing. It added a final airy flourish to the route.

In every direction stretched mountains and glaciers, intersected by channels, bays and fjords. Among embryonic sea-ice, leads of open water glinted amber in the dropping sun. Away to the south, beyond Ridge Island and the mountain-islands of Square Bay, the inviolate arrowhead of Mount Wilcox stood out above its neighbours against a sky of palest beryl. In the west, over Pourquoi Pas and a distant Adelaide, the sky was filled with reds, oranges, yellows. It was an empty, silent world, alive only in its shifting, spreading colours. Not a bird. Not even a wind. Just ourselves, alone with a dying sun, witnessing the final defiant flaring up of life that precedes extinction. And all the while the shadowline was creeping stealthily up towards our sunlit sanctuary. We lingered as long as we dared. I, for one, was reluctant to forsake, not so much the splendour of the scene, as the peace I felt in myself. Such moments of complete harmony with oneself, a companion, the universe, are all too rare ...

Then we headed swiftly downwards, delayed only at the ice-cliff where, on the bare ice, our crampons had left no traces to signpost the way over. We reached the col, to a frantic reception from the dogs, as the light faded, and raced back to camp in the dark and minus twenties, brim-full with the content that is born of a perfect day.

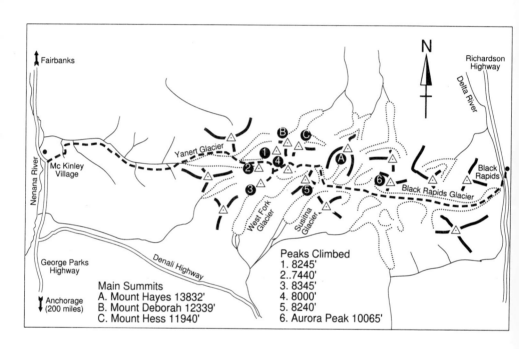

Fairbanks

Nenana River

Mc Kinley Village

Yanert Glacier

West Fork Glacier

Suslina Glacier

Black Rapids Glacier

Black Rapids

Delta River

Richardson Highway

N

George Parks Highway

Denali Highway

Anchorage (200 miles)

Peaks Climbed
1. 8245'
2..7440'
3. 8345'
4. 8000'
5. 8240'
6. Aurora Peak 10065'

Main Summits
A. Mount Hayes 13832'
B. Mount Deborah 12339'
C. Mount Hess 11940'

# A SKI TOUR IN ALASKA (1987)

We sallied forth that morning lightheartedly, revelling in the knowledge that we were fifty miles from the nearest road and off to climb our first peak. Leaving the tents up, we climbed on skins round a small ice-fall and up into a side basin of the Yanert glacier. The sun was shining and we carried only light day sacks. There was a sense of being on holiday after the hard graft of the previous week.

Almost immediately, however, the atmosphere changed. Gusts of wind swept down the basin, teasing at first, but quickly becoming vicious. The dry, loose powder that had lain so passive up to now, swirled aloft into stinging, blinding curtains of spindrift. Mike Browne and David Williams cached their skis beneath a bergschrund and swam slowly up a short but steep slope of bottomless powder. It was too cold to wait around, so Richard Cooper and I contoured round our little mountain to try our luck on another ridge. By now we could see nothing and relied for a sense of direction on the angle of our skis across the slope. Hoods up, heads turned away from the blast, we plodded on until we reached a col where, in a lull, we could dimly discern an easy rock ridge leading upwards. At that moment, Richard lost his balance and fell over. A boot released from its binding and while he struggled to relocate it, he dropped a mitt. That settled it. Summit or no summit, this was no place to be with nothing but polypro gloves on your hands. We groped our way down, skins still on the skis. My glasses were hopelessly iced-up, but I needed them to protect my eyes and had to peer over them to take advantage of the occasional lull. Mike and David caught us up, having reached the summit on their side. For a few minutes we became disorientated and strayed into a zone of crevasses. Visions of an epic began to loom before us. Wearily we climbed back uphill, then with relief, recognised a glacier trench we had followed on the way up. Soon afterwards we dropped out of the wind, and its attendant cloud of drift, and could see where we were. Off came the skins and we skied rapidly back to camp where there was scarcely a breath of wind. As we pulled clots of ice from our eyelashes, we congratulated ourselves on our choice of campsite and joked that it had been like a good day on Cairngorm — which was not, I suppose, wholly facetious. Soon we were inside the tents, brewing up. Although our faces were burning we were all chilled through and Mike was anxiously warming white, frozen toes.

We were not going to be let off so easily, however. The water had not yet boiled when the first exploratory gusts came looking for us. Within minutes we had to extinguish the stoves, and thanked our stars that we had good tents and plenty of snow on the valances. All too soon this illusion of security was dispelled. In the blasts, the roof of the tent all but touched our noses as we lay in our sleeping bags anxiously eyeing the fabric. The tent began to assume a distorted shape and we guessed that a pole had bent or snapped. One corner of the flysheet started to flap wildly, and we could feel the groundsheet lifting beneath us. The tent, it seemed, was ready for take off. Crawling out into the frenzied cloud of drift, I found more by feel than sight that the valance had been completely stripped of snow and the polythene food bags had slid off. In fact, the snow all around was being eroded away by the minute, leaving each tent perched on a pedestal. There was nothing we could do now to secure them and they were not going to last indefinitely. The battering violence of the wind made it hard not only to move but even to think, but clearly something had to be done. More by luck than judgment, we were camped a few feet from a convenient bank, where snow had drifted over a moraine ridge. While Mike and Richard knelt inside the tents, holding up the hooped poles, and no doubt holding their breath as well, at times, David and I stumbled and crawled over to the bank and frantically started to dig.

Two hours later, as it was growing dark, we had made a cave just big enough for ourselves and our belongings. Carefully, we dropped the tents, one at a time, aware that it would be only too easy to lose one. Eventually, we were all inside and the entrance blocked. After the maelstrom outside, it was miraculously still and silent. For a while, spindrift continued to pour through the chinks, but these were sealed at last. We were cramped and, when the snow in our clothing melted, very damp. Fingers throbbed as they came back to life. But we were safe from anything the elements could throw at us.

That day was a turning point in our traverse of the Hayes range. It was as though our credentials had been accepted, our entry to the high places approved. From that time on we could do no wrong ...

Six of us from the Eagle Ski Club had left George Parks highway at mile 229 eight days before, with Bob Crockett of Anchorage and his dog-team, the Chugach Express. The following day we were joined on the Yanert River by two other mushers with the rest of our food and gear. When the teams left us two days later we were on a shelf overlooking the snout of the Yanert glacier. Progress had not been as fast as we had hoped, but it had been interesting travelling with the dogs and infinitely more satisfying than an airlift. At this point Paddy O'Neill and Steve Thomas also turned back, to our deep regret and their bitter disappointment. Both had frost-bitten fingers, the result of an incident with a petrol stove, and Steve's toes were injured too. Fortunately neither suffered permanent damage. From the snout, three days of ferrying loads through Deep Soft, and one day of lie-up when it put down yet more snow, had brought us to the point where we could take a day off and try a climb.

Now, after one more day in which the wind blew itself out and we recuperated, we could enjoy ourselves. The weather became perfect, the soft snow had been replaced by wind-hardened sastrugi, and we had eaten enough to be able to move food and gear in single monster loads instead of relaying. Over the next week, we slipped into a routine of both travelling and climbing every day. There was no shortage of small peaks of modest difficulty for us to attempt. Wind-slab put a curb on our ambitions and we retreated from one route after setting off a small avalanche; but between us we reached the top of six mountains of 2500-3000 metres. These were days full of conscious pleasure and exhilaration as we skied beneath magnificent peaks like Deborah and Hess, or thankfully dropped our heavy packs and moved fast and light to the summit of the day's objective.

The key to our traverse was a col west of Mount Hayes, which was short but steep on both sides. We fixed a rope to help haul ourselves up, carrying skis as well as everything else; and for the descent in failing light on the far side, two of us preferred crampons to skis. Having crossed the col we had a not unwelcome lie-up day in heavy snow. Then the weather cleared on cue to present us with a marvellous descent in feathery powder down onto the Susitna glacier. A gentle climb brought us to the watershed where we paused a day to climb Aurora Peak by its long south-west ridge. Poling and skating energetically on a hard, fast surface, we descended the Black Rapids glacier in good style and crossed the gurgling river to reach the Richardson Highway at a sign that read: "FOOD, PHONE, GAS — 1 MILE."

The Alaska range is split in two by the George Parks Highway (and a railway line) connecting Anchorage and Fairbanks. West of the road is the McKinley National Park. East of the road lies the Hayes Range, lower and less well-known, and blissfully free from rules and regulations. It is bounded in the east by another road, the Richardson Highway, a hundred miles away as the crow flies. We knew the range to have been traversed at least once, from east to west by way of the Gillam glacier, north of Hess and Deborah. Indeed, near the snout of the Yanert, we met a party of two who had just completed that same journey. Our route, through the heart of the range had probably not been skied before as a traverse, but most sections must have been covered before by someone. To put our efforts in perspective, a few weeks after our return to Britain we heard that a party from the US nordic-ski squad had traversed the range in sixty-nine hours. Nevertheless, the area is not heavily frequented. From the Yanert snout we saw not a soul until the Black Rapids glacier, when a plane landed beside Mike as he was poling along on his own. The pilot wanted to borrow a map!

The Big Blow was a salutary reminder that Alaska is a serious place. All our reading in back numbers of the American Alpine Journal had warned us that sudden violent winds are a feature of the mountains here. Yet on only three days in three weeks could we not travel. Although we were undoubtedly lucky to have quite such good weather, past records indicate that March, April and May are the most settled months in the year. From a skier's point of view, May is too late. The rivers are breaking up and snow disappearing fast from tundra and moraine. In an admittedly very mild year, we found overflow a problem on the Yanert even at the beginning of April. Overflow is caused by water seeping up through the ice to form a surface layer of water several inches deep. At night this freezes to form sheets of smooth glare-ice, difficult to travel on. Using skins we found it even more of a problem when the ice melted in the afternoons. The last few miles of our traverse were very bare of snow. We were only able to ski all the way thanks to a raised skidoo track. The weight of the machine had compressed the snow sufficiently to withstand the thaw that was melting the rest away. All in all, March might be a safer month than April to be sure of good snow conditions low down.

March, however, is even more likely to be cold. Our arrival in Anchorage at the end of March 1986, coincided not only with the eruption of Mount Augustine and the first snow since November, but with a cold snap that lasted about a week. For the first few nights, the mercury in our little REI thermometers had dropped off the bottom of the scale at -30°C by 6pm, and must have reached -40°C at night. Towards the end of our journey we were skiing in shirtsleeves, but those first few days were colder than expected and our equipment, suitable for springtime in the Alps, was only just adequate. There was no room for error, as Paddy and Steve found to their cost.

An agent or friend in Anchorage is invaluable for a trip of this nature. We were indebted to Bob Crockett. As well as providing the dogs at a very reasonable price, he organized the hire of a van, and its return to Anchorage, at the start of our journey, and he drove all the way up to Black Rapids to bring us back to Anchorage at the end. A friend indeed.

# TWO'S COMPANY IN THE TIEN SHAN (1996)

"I love it when the most important things in my pocket are not keys and money, but lip-salve and suncream!"

The speaker was John Cousins, mountain guide and Executive Officer for the Mountain Leader Training Board, better known as JC. Four of us, all from North Wales, were camped on the snows of the upper Kayindy glacier in the Tien Shan mountains of Central Asia. We were surrounded by 5000 metre peaks, virtually all unclimbed.

To reach that spot we had flown via Istanbul and Tashkent to Alma Ata in Kazakhstan, travelled for two days through Kyrghizstan in the back of a truck, walked with porters for two days up stone-covered ice to a Base Camp and, after a couple of recces up side glaciers, had ferried loads for a further two days to our present camp.

However, our situation was rather like being in the Garden of Eden, surrounded by forbidden fruit. For our objective was Kirov Peak, 6073 metres, one of the last 6000 metre summits still unclimbed in the Tien Shan, which is in a totally different valley ... It is a remote peak, lying on the watershed of the South Inylchek and Terekty valleys with its south flank falling into China. Normally such remoteness is rendered meaningless in the Tien Shan by the use of helicopters, but, subscribing to old-fashioned values with regard to mountains, we had deliberately chosen to come out early in July, at least two weeks before the helicopters would start flying. The South Inylchek glacier is well known as the access route for Pic Pobeda 7439 metres and Khan Tengri 6995 metres, the two major peaks of the Tien Shan and much-climbed over the years. However, it seemed that climbers might never have visited the Terekty valley; certainly there was no record of any of its peaks having been climbed. It was to the Terekty, therefore, that we chose to go and we duly applied for, and received, generous grants from the Mount Everest Foundation and the Welsh Sports Council.

Why then were we camped on the Kayindy glacier, to the north of the Terekty valley? Choosing to visit little known valleys is not without hazard. Vladimir Komissarov, our likeable and efficient agent in Kyrghizstan, had always been vague about access to the Terekty. On arrival we learned that according to

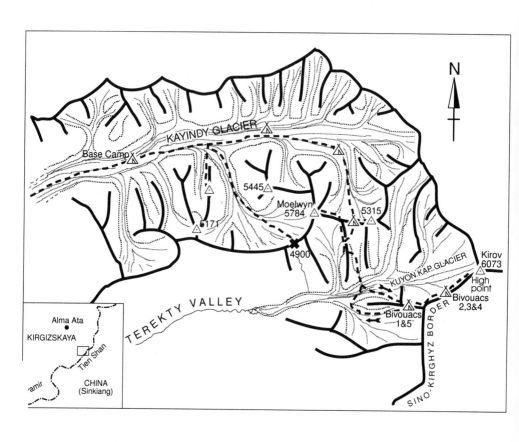

information gleaned from local hunters and the military, access on foot to the Terekty was not possible. Large sections of the old road to China, which would have to be used part of the way, had been totally destroyed by landslips, and further on a narrow gorge meant crossing and recrossing the river, a hazardous undertaking for a large party at the height of glacial melt. Access would be far easier by crossing a pass from the Kayindy, Vladimir assured us. He had been up the Terekty once in a helicopter and believed that there were several passes easy enough for porters to negotiate. In the event, this proved to be totally untrue of the upper Kayindy, whither Vladimir had led us, but at the time we were in no position to argue.

So there we were, ten days into our holiday, the porters paid off and, as yet, no sign of a route over to the Terekty or even a glimpse of Kirov Peak. It was undeniably depressing but JC and I were still optimistic. Unfortunately, our friends had become discouraged and, at this point, they succumbed to the temptations of the Kayindy. A few days later they returned to Britain.

Our relatively orthodox four-person expedition had now become a two-man venture to find the mountain as much as to climb it. The next two and a half weeks were strenuous, serious and committing. Technical difficulties were never great but the potential for disaster, be it from avalanche, cornice, crevasse, rockfall or plain carelessness was ever present and most of the time we were many days from help. For those very reasons it became a unique and deeply satisfying mountain adventure, in which success or failure on the mountain seemed almost incidental.

What follows is our diary from the time our friends decided to turn back.

*July 12*

Recce up to 5000 metre col, steep at the top. Desperately hard work, deep soft snow all the way, six hours up, two down. Inconclusive on the feasibility of a crossing but not out of the question, and we spot a good line on P.5784, the highest peak in the Kayindy basin. Seems worth putting a camp on the col. And, at last, we can see Kirov Peak. First impression is daunting, to say the least.

*July 13*

Set out for the col with monster loads but slow progress thanks to exhausting heat and collapsing steps. Camp at 4500 metres, but later, in the cool of the evening, carry a load of food and fuel to the top.

*July 14*

Old steps snowed-in overnight but still just visible, thank goodness! Up to the col and pitch the tent a little way to the west. Climb a small top to the east, P.5315. Feeling tired and camp early. Play Scrabble. JC is as interesting and entertaining in the tent as he is competent and reliable on the hill! He is also Cheyne-Stokes breathing when asleep — three deep breaths, sometimes a fourth, shallower one, over a period of ten seconds, followed by absolute silence for fifteen seconds.

*July 15*

Along the ridge carrying only day sacks for once, until we can find a way through giant cornices. Then downclimbing and traversing on ice through séracs and round bergschrunds, into a bowl beneath P.5784. Crossing the bowl we reach a spur coming down from the east ridge of the peak. It looks a safe and attractive route. Even better, below the spur a 40° snow/ice slope leads to a rock ridge and scree slopes dropping into the Terekty valley — for the first time, we know that a crossing is feasible. An enjoyable and rewarding day!

*July 16*

A change in the weather. Up till now we have experienced afternoon cloud and snow showers nearly every evening, but nothing serious and no wind. Last night *was* windy and heavy snow obliterated all our hard-won tracks. Back down to the Kayindy to pick up food and fuel sufficient for the next twelve days. Decide to make do with a single 8 mm rope and leave behind helmets and most of the rock gear. Hard slog back up to the col.

*July 17*

Along the ridge and into the bowl with single mega loads, lowering them down the steep, icy bits. Camp at the foot of the south spur of P.5784.

*July 18*

Climb the peak by way of the spur and along the east ridge. About alpine AD, with some mixed ground halfway up and a short but exciting ice-pitch through some séracs. Otherwise, a lot of deep, loose snow lying on ice and some weaving in and out of double cornices on the final ridge. Sadly, it was cloudy all day with wind and some snowfall, so little visibility and no views at all. Moelwyn — white hill in Welsh — seems a suitable name.

*July 19*

Ten pitches downclimbing the big snowslope into the Terekty valley. The snow was the usual Tien Shan combination of a thin, breakable crust over 2 foot of huge, totally unconsolidated melt-freeze grains. With heavy, unwieldy packs we pitch it all, digging deep to find ice-screw belays. Then horrible loose rock on or near the ridge crest and easier scree leading down to a complicated dry glacier. After much weaving about among crevasses, we finally camp at 3800 metres, our first night off ice for a fortnight. An exhausting day, thanks to the big packs, but at least we are now in the right valley!

*July 20*

We treat ourselves to a rest day before the big effort that will be needed on Kirov Peak. We cannot see the col immediately North of Kirov and do not have the time or food for a recce in that direction. Instead, we are opting for the west spur which leads to the south-west ridge. It will be an immensely long route but appears reasonably straightforward. Success will depend on favourable snow conditions and weather, and on moving fast; but we are fit and acclimatized now and, touch wood, the weather around here never seems to become *really* bad.

*July 21*

Set off with five days food. A perfect morning, but the weather deteriorates from midday onwards. Descend onto the Kuyon-Kap glacier at 3600 metres and cross it; then up loose scree and a big open ice slope to the crest of the west spur. Purple saxifrage in flower on the scree seems a good omen but higher up a rock, dislodged by John's dangling ice-axe loop on a short pitch, hits me at the bottom of my back. Painful — my involuntary gasps and groans cause John to climb rapidly back down — but no serious injury. Food for thought, nevertheless!

Over a satellite summit at the junction of north and west spurs, and bivi not far beyond, using the Quasar flysheet and ski poles very effectively to make a bivi tent.

*July 22*

Fresh snow overnight and much rumbling of thunder in the distance. Up to the junction with the main south-west ridge via a couple of ice pitches and a lot of exhausting, unconsolidated snow. Brief view of enormous cornices leading to Kirov and wide easy-angled glaciers on the Chinese side before the weather closes in. Along the ridge in wind, snow and poor visibility; at first on hard ice for several rope lengths on the Chinese side, moving together with ice-screw runners; then on the West, or Kyrghiz side, to stay on top of the cornices. Pitch the fly on a flat section at about 5300 metres

*July 23*

A stormy night. Despite snow blocks all round the fly, everything at each end is buried under inches of spindrift and there is a continuous shower of hoar frost as the wind shakes the walls. Thank goodness for goretex bivi bags! At 5am a start is out of the question. At 8am there is a lull and a slight clearing so we brew up and get dressed, only for the weather to clamp down again. Moving along such a heavily corniced ridge in zero visibility is not an option, so we dig a snow cave to make ourselves more comfortable, at least, and move in. Brew up, sleep and play desert island discs. We cannot afford this lost day. Tomorrow will have to be exceptional in terms of both weather and effort ...

*July 24*

Weather still poor but some visibility. We set out with one light sack between us, conscious that this will be our only chance of reaching the summit. A trying day ... Long traverses on steep slopes over huge drops down the north-west face, pockets of soft slab alternating with the usual bottomless melt-freeze crystals. Visibility comes and goes but we never see the summit. We give cornice edges a wide berth, or so we think, until on one flat section, a place where we would confidently have pitched a tent, a huge segment ten metres deep and fifty metres long suddenly breaks away. John has just taken over breaking trail and, relaxing after mental as well as physical strain, I am plodding along in his footsteps, brain in neutral, when it happens. The fracture line is between my feet, though John is on terra firma with the rope tight. I dangle for a moment from my ice-axe, thrust instinctively into the snow; then, amazingly, a small section of the cornice which has failed to break off swings back like a rat-trap to imprison me from the waist down. It all happens too quickly to be frightening and, but for the pressure on my legs, it would be almost comic. I am carrying the shovel in the sack on my back so, while John anchors the rope downslope, I start digging. It takes ten minutes, with cautious help from John, to release myself.

The mountain seems to be telling us something, but we don't want to give up yet and continue, albeit in chastened mood. However, after six hours climbing the weather is becoming steadily worse and we are still on the horizontal section of the ridge. We have a brief glimpse of yet more gigantic cornices ahead and know that beyond them there is still 600 metres vertical height, of unknown technical difficulty, to be gained. Suddenly it seems too far and too much. We have done our utmost but yesterday's wasted day has stymied us. Reluctantly, but with a strong sense that we are not welcome on this mountain, we turn back.

*July 25*

Retreat in a storm — snow, wind and swirling spindrift, very cold, very Scottish, but no Red Burn to make for ... With little food left and slab avalanche conditions developing, we cannot afford to sit it out. Dangerous and exhausting climbing along the ridge, clearing away the newly-formed slab before taking each sideways step, belaying all the way. Then down the spur, setting off a big slab near the top. Downclimb the first little ice-pitch where a sérac wall abuts the ridge crest, but sacrifice an ice-screw to abseil the start of the next one. Intrigued to find well-developed depth-hoar crystals at the bottom of the snow-pack while excavating for a belay. Late in the day we reach the site of our first bivi, the worst now behind us.

*July 26*

The mountain lets us off the hook! Good weather at last. No breakfast, but we find an easy alternative descent on the south side of the spur, then an improbable but straightforward route beside the glacier all the way down to a moraine shelf where we can brew up and dry out in sunshine. Easily down to the valley, revelling in warmth and familiar alpine flowers — purple and orange asters, yellow rock-rose and creamy rock-jasmine. On the lateral moraine of the valley glacier, to our astonishment, we stumble across a solitary cairn; no more than one stone on top of another, on a boulder, but an unmistakable sign that someone has been here before. Not really surprising, and in our situation it is poignant rather than disappointing, for we are still a very long way from Base Camp, let alone other people. Wearily — and hungrily — we plod back up to our food-dump.

*July 27*

Heavy snow all night but clears during the morning and we are away just after midday, feeling sluggish and lethargic. The glacier is scary, with crevasses masked by several inches of new snow. Carelessly, I drop a ski pole while probing and it disappears with a tinkling sound of breaking icicles. Slowly, we toil up steep, unstable scree which becomes slightly easier as the new snow deepens towards the top. We pitch the tent right on the crest of the sharp ridge dropping from Pik Moelwyn, at the foot of the big snow slope. Memorable views across to Kirov and the icy sérac-laden faces of peaks to the west, but not a place for sleep-walking!

*July 28*

Back up the snow slope, the ubiquitous crust bearing our weight for some of the time, at least, otherwise we might never have escaped the Terekty valley. Once in the bowl beneath Moelwyn, however, the snow is soft and deep and the heat enervating. After covering three hundred yards in an hour we abandon the packs and put in a set of tracks up onto the ridge, unladen. That done, we pitch the inner tent and spend the afternoon brewing and sleeping. At 4pm we pack up and climb easily onto the ridge in cooler conditions. Along the ridge, still in deep powder but feeling strong again now, invigorated by glorious evening sunlight and valedictory views of Kirov and the Terekty valley. Even the cornices, icicles dripping like fangs from their jaws, seem almost friendly now we are saying farewell. A bitter little wind substitutes freezing fingers for such sentiment as we don crampons and the rope to negotiate an ice-step and some nasty-feeling slab at the top of the Kayindy slope. Down, labouring through a crust that is breakable but only just, into the reds and oranges of sunset. Finally camp as light fades at 9pm and cook by torchlight.

*July 29*

Out of food now, but we quickly descend the side glacier on a crust that is breakable at first (oh no! not again!) but miraculously improves as we lose height. Coffee and biscuits in the sun at the kit-bag of food where we said goodbye to our friends all that time ago, in another lifetime it seems. Then we add the contents of the cache to our rucksacks to bring them back to the regulation 30kg and head down the glacier.

For the first time in days I have time to reflect. Although we have not climbed Kirov, I feel utterly content. Our names will not go down in the record books but I shall remember these three weeks as one of the best of times with one of the best of companions. One of Tilman's wise sayings springs to mind:

> 'A man ought to rate his achievements only by the satisfaction they give him, for they will soon be outdone, outshone and speedily forgotten by everyone but himself.'

I rate our Tien Shan sojourn very highly indeed.

A circling helicopter is the first indication that civilization may be closer than expected. Soon afterwards we meet two British climbers, just arrived, and hear about the double tragedy on P.5445 in which first Mick Davie and then two Russian guides died in cornice accidents. Mindful of our own experience,

I can only reflect that 'There but for the Grace of God go I'.

Although no part of our plans, or desires, we find ourselves being flown out a few hours later, along with the two porters who had come to meet us and the Russian rescue team who have been on the mountain. The helicopter struggles to get off the ground, initially because the chocks have not been removed from the wheels, but mainly because it is overladen for that altitude (eighteen people on board, plus a great deal of equipment). I find it the most alarming moment of the trip when the pilot finally gains enough height to accelerate forward, skimming only inches from the ground for two hundred metres.

It is a sombre ride in that roaring, vibrating machine. The Russians are subdued, eyes downcast. I have my feet on the bundles of rope and tarpaulin on the floor of the helicopter until John nudges me. Aghast, I realize that the bundles are actually the bodies of the two Russian guides. A hand is sticking out of one of them. It is a strange, sad end to our journey.

# The Himalaya

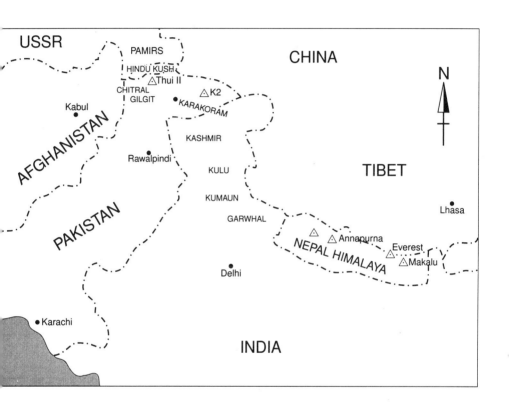

# CHITRAL 1969

"Salaam Alaikum," I call.

"Alaikumus Salam," replies a proud-looking horseman, courteously reining in. He is dressed in a blue shirt worn outside baggy white pantaloons and a white beret that can be rolled down over the ears in winter. His features could easily be European. Behind walks a servant carrying two polo sticks and a small bundle containing both their belongings. He is a well-to-do Chitrali, off to a polo match three days' ride away. Polo is the national sport of Chitral; every village has its own carefully tended pitch and any Chitrali of substance will own a polo pony. The annual match between Chitral and Gilgit, held on the Shandhur Pass at 3700 metres is the social event of the year for several thousand square miles of mountain country.

But where and what is Chitral? A province on the northern border of Pakistan, separated from Russia only by the twenty-mile strip of Afghan territory known as the Wakhan Corridor, it is alien to the rest of Pakistan in both language and racial characteristics. Last August, Chitral was incorporated into Pakistan, ending four hundred years of rule by an autocratic royal family. Prince Buhan-ud-din, one of the senior members of the family, entertained us to lunch and, over mutton pilau and home-made wine, aired his views on the need for enlightened despotism — with himself as despot. Access to Chitral is difficult: air flights are scheduled three times a week but cloud over the Lawowri Pass (3000 metres) frequently prevents the aircraft from getting through. The alternative is to drive the 150 miles of rough road from Rawalpindi to Dir and there to hire a jeep. The seventy miles from Dir to Chitral took us ten and a half hours, much of the time in four-wheel drive. The pass is only open for three months of the year. Large streams flow over and along the road at random; in places it cuts straight through permanent snowfields. Once we had to wait while a rock fall was cleared away. Three-point turns are necessary on most of the hairpin bends and every time the driver changes gear his mate has to jump off to place a chock behind the wheels. Beyond Chitral town the road continues for twenty miles; thereafter the only mode of travel is on foot or horseback.

The Chitralis are open-handed, friendly and honest. Europeans still arouse

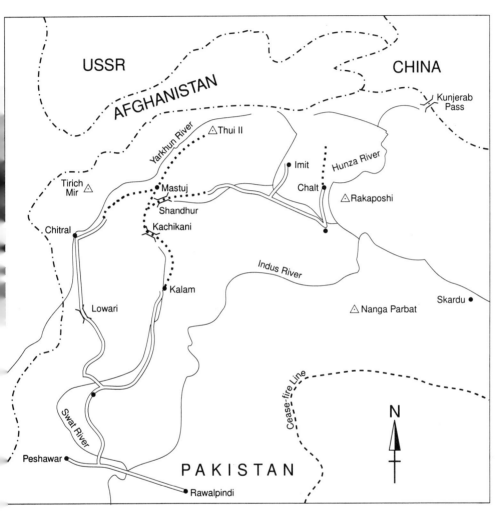

This map also refers to the article "Summer in Gilgit" on p125

curiosity though mountaineers and hippies are visiting the country in increasing numbers (hashish is both plentiful and legal): yet it is a polite curiosity, neither importuning not obsequious as so often in the East. All along our route we were offered platefuls of delicious apricots and cups of sweet milky tea (water and goats' milk in equal quantities are heated up along with the tea-leaves and stewed for ten minutes. Flavoured by wood-smoke, the result is nothing like English tea, but still delicious and very nourishing. In remoter villages, sugar is unobtainable and instead the tea is stirred with a lump of rock salt). Apricots grow everywhere in the villages along with mulberries, grapes, walnuts and tiny crisp apples. The villages are little oases scattered along the valley-bottoms of steep, barren mountains and after a dusty walk under a scorching sun, they seem like paradise, with their fruit, shade, green grass and clear tinkling streams. It is hard to imagine that this idyll exists only for three months of the year and that for the rest, life is a harsh struggle against the cold. I suspect, however, that in mid-winter hashish and mulberry wine help to induce a state of near hibernation ...

I am writing this under a tree in the little village of Wasam, more than a hundred miles from Chitral up the main Yarkhun valley, while I wait for the other members of our grandly titled British Hindu Raj Expedition to arrive. A week ago, Dick Isherwood and I set out to reconnoitre a possible approach to our mountain, Thui II (6524 metres), leaving Chris Wood and Colin Taylor, together with our pompous, overweight liaison officer Major Munawar Khan, to follow on with donkeys carrying our food and equipment. Four days ago Dick developed bad blisters on both feet and I was forced to go on alone. Reaching Wasam, I hired a local man to guide me to the Thui An, a pass of 4500 metres from which our mountain is visible. He was a little fellow with a quizzical expression whose only concessions to the mountains were a blanket round the shoulders and goatskins on his feet. It was a long day, the last section over jumbled boulders, wading swift icy streams and up a dry-ice glacier. We reached the top as the sun was setting, watched by a solitary ibex with huge, swept-back horns. It was an exciting moment, for though the pass is used fairly frequently by the locals, it can have been crossed by few, if any, Europeans. Stretched before us was a panorama of magnificent mountains which had been mere names before, Thui II most prominent of all. We spent the night there, on a small island of shingle in the snow, huddled together for warmth in a large polythene bag. It was not comfortable and we had little to eat, but I was too exhilarated to care. Next day, we stopped at the first hut we came across to celebrate on boiled chicken garnished with sugar ...

The news I have for the others is not encouraging, however. From this side the mountain looks formidable; we will have to try the alternative approach from the north, but it seems that Thui II is going to be difficult from any direction.

* * * * *

Advanced Base is two small orange tents on a patch of snow among some boulders. The snow is melting rapidly and already the tents are isolated on foot-high pedestals. A matter of feet away is the Shetor Glacier, a chaotic jumble of ice twelve miles long and a mile wide, leading into the heart of the largely unexplored Hindu Raj mountains. The glacier has never been visited before. Every now and then, a poised block of ice collapses with a crash or a stone-fall roars down the mountainside, leaving a plume of dust and ugly scars in the snow. One night we were wakened by a rasping crunch as a boulder weighing several tons slid from its perch on the glacier to within three feet of the tent. Mysterious creaks and groans sound from below us. It is not a peaceful camp.

At 15,000 feet we are half way up the glacier. From a Base Camp in the valley 5000 feet below, it has taken twelve days of reconnaissance and load-carrying to establish ourselves here. Colin and I have climbed a peak of about 5300 metres immediately behind the camp. The route looked deceptively short from below and we were slowed down more than we had expected by altitude, so that our 'day off' took us eleven hours, up one AD ridge of slabby granite blocks and down another. It got dark on the way down. Colin is very short-sighted and unfortunately on this occasion he had only his dark glasses ... We are dangerously late in the season. We have been warned that after August 15th the weather is likely to be unsettled and the winter snows could set in any day. It is now August 10th. On top of a nine-day walk-in, we have been delayed over two weeks by the machinations of Major Munawar Khan who spends much of his time composing telegrams to the government begging that we be prevented from climbing. Liaison Officers have to be fully equipped for altitudes up to at least 8000 metres. Sadly, Major Munawar prefers to lie on a charpoy while his batman brings him cups of tea and cuts his toenails. Batman even follows him into the bushes every morning, carrying the bog-roll. We are not friends.

Nevertheless, surrounded by such superb mountains, morale cannot be anything but high. Crawling through the sleeve-entrance of our tents in the morning, we look straight across the Yarkhun valley to the mountains of the Afghan Hindu Kush, twenty miles away. Turning to look up the glacier, Thui II stands out immediately. Dr. Gerald Gruber saw the mountain from the valley floor two years ago. In an article in the Alpine Journal he wrote, "In my opinion it is the most beautiful and isolated summit in the Hindu Kush or Hindu Raj". Now, only a mile from the foot of its East Ridge, we can thoroughly endorse his words; the mountain is magnificent. And difficult, too. Dr. Gruber in his article went on to say: "The ascent of Thui II will require a strong team and a massive outlay of equipment." We hope we are a strong team but we have chosen to ignore the latter part of this warning. We prefer to attempt the mountain alpine-style, a small mobile party travelling self-contained and as far as possible doing away with permanent camps. Unfortunately, both the ridges visible to us are extremely long and bristling with difficulties. Either would mean so many nights on the mountain that bivouacking is out of the question, which is presumably what Dr. Gruber meant. Yet we simply do not have the fixed-rope and other gear to embark on siege tactics. However, we are putting our faith in the old mountaineering adage, "There's always an easy way round the back". While Colin and I attempt a smaller peak nearby, Dick and Chris are going to the far end of the glacier to find it.

Colin and I climbed our mountain. It was about 6000 metres and gave us a long day's climbing from a light camp at 5100 metres. We called it Pachan Zom, the Hidden Mountain, since it is not shown on the map and, except from one point on the glacier, it is completely concealed by intervening peaks and spurs. The closer look it gave us at Thui's north-east ridge merely confirmed the impression that it was definitely not an alpine route.

Dick and Chris had better news. Bivouacking twice at the head of the glacier, they climbed a straightforward snow-peak of 5600 metres on their first day and from there could see that the mountain's south ridge was far more feasible than the other two. Of prime importance, it was much shorter — could we but place a camp on the obvious col at 5800 metres. The problem was to reach the col. The only route to it was up a slope dissected by enormous bergschrunds and apparently threatened by séracs. On their second day, however, Dick and Chris found a way through that was quite safe, if spectacular, the key being an exciting traverse along the lower lip of a bergschrund.

Forthwith, all four of us set off up the glacier carrying tents, climbing gear and food for six days. It was 17th August. We spent the night at 5200 metres and the following day picked our way through the bergschrunds to a sheltered bowl just beneath the col where we set up a camp. We were all set to climb the mountain.

It was not to be, however. The sky had been overcast all day and during the night it began to snow. When we awoke not even the col was visible. Snow was softly settling over the tent, swiftly and silently burying us. For the next two days Chris and I lived in a state of suspended animation within the stuffy orange world of our tent, scarcely aware that the other two still existed.

The third day was bright and clear. Far away we could see Rakaposhi. The new snow was dazzling, even through goggles, but on the rock above it was vanishing before our eyes as the sun reached it. Kicking through the fresh snow to névé beneath, we quickly front-pointed the 100 metres to the col and started up the rock. It was granite, at first loose and shattered, but becoming firmer; and before long we were enjoying fine slabby climbing of about IV with the occasional strenuous ice-choked chimney. Colin even found himself a bit of V. Above, the ridge narrowed and there was interesting mixed climbing, with several little ice-pitches. We seemed to have been climbing a long time, but altitude and heavy sacks full of bivi gear had slowed us down and our actual height gain was not very great. The angle eased, and emerging from behind two gigantic rock pillars which from below we had nicknamed 'The Rabbit's Ears', we saw the ridge stretching before us. We were at about 6100 metres; there was still 400 metres to go, but after the next 60 metres it looked like a snow-plod.

However, it would soon be dark and the Rabbit's Ears was the last sheltered site for a bivouac. We decided to stop there. With luck, we should be able to reach the summit and return to camp the same day. Jubilant at having all but climbed the peak, we settled down for the night. Dick and Colin found a perfect two-man cave twenty feet down a shaft that separated an enormous cornice from the rock. Chris and I made ourselves at home in a little hollow, with one of the Ears at our backs.

With pits, duvets and a bivi sack, we were quite snug. We were so warm in fact, it was ominous. I felt drowsy but could not actually sleep. Time passed. All at once, I became aware of a cold, wet sensation at the back of my neck. It was snowing; and it continued to do so all night. The bivi sack was hopelessly small. I am 5 feet 8 inches tall and had difficulty in keeping my head covered; Chris is 6 feet 6 inches. The night passed in a restless tug-of-war.

Daybreak was a faint lightening of the gloom. The usual epics with clumsy mitts and frozen ropes and crampon straps. Chilled and stiff, we slowly started to climb, trying to postpone a decision. The wind was rising and it was very cold. It had stopped snowing, but a temporary lifting of the clag only showed more clouds rolling down the glacier towards us. We turned back. The weather had arrived just a day too early. Bitterly we thought of those wasted weeks in the valley.

The descent took most of the day. The rock had disappeared under a foot of snow and we had to abseil all the way; just like Observatory Ridge last March. After the final abseil, inevitably, the rope jammed. The cold had caused rope and hemp loop to freeze together and both had frozen in a solid lump to the rock. I climbed back up an icy slab to free it and naturally, a crampon strap broke ...

There was still the final slope of névé to descend, treacherous now with thick soft snow lying over it. Through a parting in the mist we could see the tents only 100 metres below. Carefully we climbed down till we reached the wide bergschrund which on the way up we had crossed some way to the left. Traversing a safe 10 metres above it, Chris headed for the bridge. Suddenly he gave a yell. His crampons had balled up and one foot had slid from beneath him. The next instant he was tobogganing over the edge of the bergschrund. With a jerk the rope came tight around the axe I had hammered in as an afterthought. Faintly I heard a voice calling. Then the strain came off the rope and Chris appeared. He had shot straight over the bergschrund landing 5 metres below as he came onto the rope. Five minutes later we were crawling into the tent, while outside the snow came down harder than ever.

Back at Advanced Base the weather remained bad, and our time was up. Nevertheless, we decided to give it one more try if the weather improved at all. Returning to Base Camp for more food, however, we were greeted by a beaming Liaison Officer with the news that our permission to climb the mountain had been rescinded by the government. We spent the next five days writing statements for an official enquiry into the affair; no less a person than the Colonel Commandant of the Chitral Scouts had come galloping up the valley on horseback to conduct it. My reconnaissance to the Thui An was the pretext, but injured pride was the real problem.

After this, Munawar Khan wisely travelled down the valley on his own. That he had not starved while we were away on the mountain became evident when we were compelled to pay a food bill for £120. A chicken costs two shillings in Chitral.

I have never hated anyone as much as I hated Munawar Khan, and the feeling was clearly mutual. When we finally came to leave Pakistan we were turned back at the Khyber Pass on his instructions and forced to spend a further week in Rawalpindi, explaining some poorly concealed blackmarket transactions. Later I learned that it had taken considerable diplomatic effort to save me from a Pakistani jail. I suppose you could say he had the last laugh.

# HIMALAYAN GRANDE COURSE (1974)

Moonlight upon a glacier. Two figures picking their separate ways over the ice. Two minds conscious of frozen beauty in the silent black and silver mountainscape, but dwelling more perhaps on cold oats settling heavily in their stomachs. Overhead, rock looms higher, casting a cold forbidding shadow far across the glacier. Into its chilly embrace, reluctantly, with a sense of the irrevocable; up an avalanche cone encrusted with fallen stones thickly as the sky above with stars; by devious bridges over a bergschrund; to stand at last peering up the streak of grey ice which is the slip-road to the face above. A typical alpine situation.

Not the Alps, however, but the Himalaya. The lesser Himalaya certainly — the mountain is only just over 6000 metres high, and from a distance, its broad, wedge-shaped south face, 900 metres of striated, almost snow-free rock, reminds one of the Dolomites. No icy giant, but the Himalaya nonetheless; the South Parbati region of Kulu in Northern India, to be precise.

Twenty-five years ago, Tom Longstaff, possibly the most widely travelled of all Himalayan climbers, wrote à propos Everest: "I hope and believe that one day it will be climbed. Then when no higher 'altitude record' is possible, mountaineers can turn to the true enjoyment of the Himalaya, most likely to be found at about 20,000 ft or less." For most climbers it is not the height that makes the Himalaya so attractive, not once they have experienced altitude. Leaving aside the special fascination of the valleys with their ancient trade-routes, simple, contented people, and exotic flora and fauna, it is the fact that climbers can be, must be, self-sufficient. By inclination, I am an alpinist — Harrison's Rocks appal me, the south ridge of Everest attracts me, if anything, even less. Yet, except in winter, the Alps are being reduced to the status of outcrops, albeit serious ones. The alpinist must look elsewhere for a wholly satisfying test of his skill and judgment. And while the great peaks of the Himalaya still tend to demand not so much skill and speed as endurance and tenacity, the more so the harder the route, the lower peaks do provide such a test.

Dick Isherwood, Geoff Cohen and John Cardy must have thought something similar, for I had little difficulty in persuading them to come. The previous day Geoff and I had climbed a fine ice-face, resembling the Tour Ronde in length and difficulty. And now Dick and I were attempting the big, nameless rock peak which dominated our particular glacier.

Dick, who does not like ice, has described the initial couloir thus: "The next four pitches were for me the most thrilling part of the climb. The dark grey section of the couloir was ice with bits of rock stuck into it, and was not too well frozen. I persuaded Rob to put a rope on and followed him up a shallow waterfall running in the central groove. Fortunately the moon was full, so I could see the small, bird-like marks left by his axe and hammer. I stuck my weapons into the same holes, but even my Chouinard hammer did not seem to work properly, and I was thankful for the occasional rock big enough to pull on. I was very glad when even Rob decided that the gully was getting steep, and we traversed to the rock just before dawn."

We had timed it perfectly. As we traversed ice-coated slabs to a terrace running the breadth of the face, the sun began to caress the skyline above, and minutes later the first stones were clattering down the couloir. Below us now lay a blanket of cloud, smothering the glacier and the camp on its edge; above the cloud stood the mountains we had climbed and were to climb, the 17,000 ft col we had crossed to get there and the summits of a myriad other peaks stretching away into the crystal distances of China and Garwhal. It was another perfect day.

Our satisfaction was short-lived, however. As Dick started up steep rock from the terrace, weaving an improbable but, in the event, fairly straightforward way through a maze of little roofs, stones in ones and twos came bounding down the face itself. The climbing above was not sustained, in fact there were several sections of scrambling, but in places the rock was loose, with the looseness of tottering blocks stacked on top of each other, and increasingly frequent whines, thuds and crashes kept our nerves on edge. The stones flurried me more than Dick. "They're only small and small ones can't do much damage," he commented. I was impressed by his calm, but unconvinced by his reasoning. However, retreat would be no safer, so I pinned my hopes on the theory that most of the stones were coming from Snow-patch Terrace — another broad terrace about halfway up the face where a solitary pitch of snow had lingered providing a conspicuous landmark.

Hurrying from relatively sheltered rib to rib, belaying where possible under overhangs, we made good time and by mid-morning were sitting at the top of the terrace, watching little stones, freed from their casing of ice, topple over, roll slowly to the edge and disappear on their long journey to the glacier. With our backs to a smooth grey wall, gaudily streaked with yellow and plumb vertical, we felt safe from above. But where now? The only two visible lines would clearly need much pegging, not at all to our taste though we had the gear for it. The wall stretched across the face, a good 300 feet high, unrelenting in its steepness. The only hope lay in a recess some way to our left, into which we could not see. Suddenly a pebble arrived beside us with a smack. Dick didn't turn a hair but the place had lost its charm for me and I could not start climbing again too quickly. Traversing left along a sharp rim of ice, where the snow patch lapped against the rock, using it now for hands, now for feet, delicate without axe or crampons, I found the recess to contain a long scoop slanting back rightwards. The angle, compared with the sheer walls on either side, looked easy. "It's a piece of duff," I yelled, promptly discovering that the difference was only relative. Breathless and out of balance, I found myself lunging for resting places which vanished as I reached them. Moreover, the holds were covered with a fine rubble which, it occurred to me briefly, could only have come from above. Predictably, the rope came tight in the midst of my struggles. Luckily, a sense of urgency must have been communicated down the rope, for although he could not hear me, Dick unbelayed, enabling me to climb a few feet higher to a good foothold which would serve as a stance. Dick had climbed over me and, with the aid of a couple of pegs, had emerged onto an easier slab when, with a whistle, a salvo of rocks came down right on top of us. There was a rattling on my helmet and something large gave me a nudge as it passed between me and the rock. I gripped the rope tighter waiting for a weight to come on it. Nothing happened; Dick, to my surprise, was unhurt. Nevertheless, even he must have been shaken, for he shot up the rest of that pitch to a friendly overhang, and when I next saw him his sharp features seemed to have become slightly sharper, though he said nothing. For my part, I peered upwards with great care, before scurrying over the exposed slab. Fortunately, I could see an apparently sheltered line slanting rightwards for at least the next run-out. I say fortunately, because otherwise I would not have continued and, as it turned out, that was the last time stonefall was to bother us until the descent.

At the end of my pitch the rock was once more vertical and I was wondering if it could possibly go free, when I noticed that Dick had disappeared. Investigating a lower line, he had come to a hole beneath some blocks; ever curious, he took off his sack and crawled through it to discover an overhung but easy-angled ramp cutting through the verticality. This proved to be the key to the wall and in effect to the whole climb. The only bulge was well-endowed with jugs and at its top, we were on easy broken ground. The chimney-line which formed the continuation of our original couloir was only a rope-length to our right, and not far above was the crest of the east ridge, where presumably nothing solid could fall on us. We were at about 5800 metres and for the first time could allow ourselves to feel confident of success. Suddenly, to our amazement, we spotted a white rope hanging down the chimney. Later we learnt that it had been left the previous year by an unsuccessful party from the University of Aston; but at the time it took the wind out of our sails to discover climbing litter on 'our' virgin mountainside.

Following the line of least resistance leftwards, it was several more rope-lengths before we reached a snow shoulder on the ridge and could look down upon a new glacier and across at new peaks. Disappointment seemed to have reduced our impetus though we had, we were surprised to find, been on the go for fourteen hours. Either way, a brew was called for. The usual afternoon cloud was swirling up and sweaters and windproofs were pulled on hurriedly in a sharp flurry of snow. It did not last, however, and through windows in the mist we could see the ridge rising up above in a monolith of orange granite, its east side sheer and almost featureless, the south face equally compact but set back in a sweep of comfortably angled slabs.

Morale improved by the cup of tea, we descended a little snow slope to a notch in the ridge and set off up the slabs. The climbing was glorious in golden evening sunlight, the cloud still boiling about the smaller peaks but dropping just enough to leave us unmolested. Big holds were few and far between but the rock was so rough that it sliced open finger tips, and was covered with tiny knobs and pockets on which bendy boots felt like PA's. Only once, when, leaning sideways from a peg, I swung across in a committing mantelshelf over a short wall onto a slab steeper and smoother than usual, was the climbing hard enough to preclude conscious enjoyment of every moment. One stance, squatting beneath a long square-cut roof, reminded me or Rebuffat's route on the Midi, and the climbing was not dissimilar to that of the famous 'Red Slab'.

Two pitches higher we came to the ideal bivouac site, complete with icicles, tucked away in a shady niche, for water. There wasn't room for two side by side, so we took separate apartments, Dick excavating himself a coffin-like trench, while I built up a platform of flat blocks, taking care to add a parapet. The Hilton had nothing on that bivouac. Not that it mattered, we were tired enough to sleep anywhere. It had been a long day, and though the climbing had been easier than expected, it had had its moments all the same, altitude tending to make difficulties feel perhaps a grade harder than they would in the Alps. We were carrying sleeping bags rather than duvets and slept the clear windless night through, not bothering with the bivi sack.

After luxuriating in our bags until the sun came up next morning, three rope-lengths of the same superb slab-climbing brought us to the summit ridge. This was snow, rimming the rocky face like froth on top of a pint. Almost horizontal, rising very gently to its highest point about 200 metres away, it was also sharply corniced, so that far from being the football field we had half expected, it was more like a screwdriver. A few minutes later, one at a time because of the cornice, we were on top, letting our eyes sweep slowly round through 360 degrees of mountains. On every side lay a parched brown landscape splashed with grey, turbulent and empty. Neither welcoming nor hostile, it was unmindful of us, waiting thirstily for the winter snows.

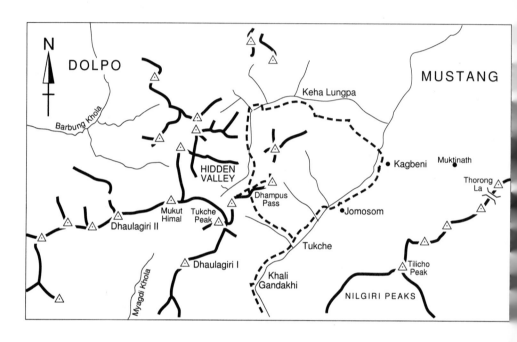

DOLPO

MUSTANG

Keha Lungpa

Barbung Khola

HIDDEN
VALLEY

Dhampus
Pass

Kagbeni

Muktinath

Thorong
La

Mukut
Himal

Tukche
Peak

Jomosom

Dhaulagiri II

Myagdi Khola

Dhaulagiri I

Tukche

Khali
Gandakhi

Tilicho
Peak

NILGIRI PEAKS

114

# THE HIDDEN VALLEY (1974)

From a distance, the little town of Tukche resembles some desert fort, with its flat roofs and windowless, seemingly continuous whitewashed walls. As one approaches it becomes apparent that the town is, in fact, split by a narrow cobbled street. On either side of it carved wooden doorways open onto courtyards where horses are tethered and women weave gaudily-dyed wools. Apart from this street, the walls are indeed almost continuous and it is possible to walk from end to end of the town over the rooftops, stepping around fruit or grain spread out to dry. The likeness to a fort is not illusory, Early in the nineteenth century the local Thakali merchants were granted by the Gorkha kings of Nepal a monopoly of the salt trade with Tibet, and since virtually all salt has to be imported into Nepal, they waxed fat on the proceeds. Until the Chinese seizure of Lhasa in 1959 Tukche was the chief centre for this trade, and the solid two-storeyed houses, each looking inwards onto its own courtyard were both storehouses for salt and grain, and strongholds to withstand marauding bandits from Tibet or jealous rivals from the chain of petty castle kingdoms further north. Today, the richer merchants have transferred their activities to pastures new. Only occasionally does the mellifluous clanging of deep-toned bells herald the arrival of a mule-train, which usually does not bother to stop. Although all the houses are occupied, some by Tibetan refugees, the town wears a forlorn, forgotten aspect and its main street seems unnaturally silent and deserted.

But even if it is reduced to a shadow of its former glory, the geographical position of the town still renders it significant. To the east, on the far side of a broad alluvial plain of stone and sand, where the great cleft cut by the Kali Gandaki river widens out, the magnificent ice wall of the Nilgiri peaks dominates the valley. To the west steep pine-clad slopes rise up to Tukche peak, the northernmost outlier of the Dhaulagiri range. In effect one is emerging from a defile between the Annapurna and Dhaulagiri massifs and, were it permitted, only four more days' walking would bring one to Mustang and the Central Asian Plateau. One of the easiest Himalayan passes, the course of the Kali Gandaki is an ancient trade route on which Tukche occupies a pivotal position. Not only strategically, but also climatically and culturally, it can be seen as a doorway between the very different worlds of India and Tibet.

Climatically, the town lies in the rain shadow of Dhaulagiri: its flat roofs and the small area under cultivation are symptoms of the dryness of the climate. In contrast to the luxuriant, semi-tropical forests further south, here even the pines and junipers are beginning to thin out and by Marpha, less than two hours' walk beyond, trees have all but disappeared. All the year round, strong winds blow up and down the valley, banging shutters and rattling doors, and raising clouds of dust which make travel uncomfortable. Culturally, the Chorten gateway on the north side of the town — a typical feature of nearly every Buddhist village — is the first to be met as one travels up from the south. Passing beneath the frescoes, albeit faded and cracked, painted on the inside of the archway, one is not just leaving the town but leaving behind an Indian-orientated Hinduism and entering the sphere of Tibetan Buddhism. Although the division, be it between climates or cultures, is obviously far from clearcut, the Chorten gateway of Tukche is nevertheless a significant symbol for travellers like ourselves.

We reached it in the middle of October My wife, Netti, and I had flown to Kathmandu where David Gundry, an old climbing friend, was waiting for us. A bus journey to Pokhara, eighty miles west of Kathmandu, and six days walking northwards through spectacular mountain scenery brought us, together with four porters and sufficient food for a month, to Tukche. Our immediate objective was the Dhampus Pass, 5000 metres, and the so-called Hidden Valley to which it gives access. This name is not entirely fanciful, since the existence of the valley was not even suspected until the French mountaineering expedition of 1950, investigating the approaches to Dhaulagiri, stumbled upon it. The Dhampus Pass is the only easy way into it. Once inside, we hoped to explore the valley and climb any peaks that were within our scope. Others had visited the Hidden Valley before us, but as we knew next to nothing about their activities, and only the most rudimentary of maps are obtainable in Nepal, a sense of exploration could be maintained.

The first day of the long haul from Tukche up to the Pass took us through pine-forests and over the pastures beyond, on a path strewn with gentians, forget-me-nots, and a myriad flowers whose names we did not know. Briefly, as we emerged onto the uplands, we could gaze northwards over the wide desert landscape of Mustang, startling in its impression of limitless space after the confines of the Kali Gandaki. Subtle variations in pink, yellow and ochre magically enlivened a theme of dusty brown, and beyond it, like a layer of cloud, stretched the snowcapped plateau of Tibet. All too quickly the view disappeared as we were enfolded by the mountains, but there were compensations in the beautifully fluted ice of Tukche Peak's north face, and in our first encounter with yaks. Larger and shaggier editions of Highland Cattle, a herd was still grazing at 4000 metres despite the lateness of the year, and would not be brought down until the winter snows arrived in earnest.

At this stage we were not alone. A group of Frenchmen, four of them professional guides on holiday with three Sherpas, twelve porters, and two hundredweight of specially imported French sausage and cheese, set off from Tukche on the same morning as ourselves. By mistake three of them, instead of following the normal yak-herders path, took a more circuitous and difficult route which only brought them to the pastures as night fell. Unfortunately our porters, following the wrong set of sahibs, went with them. They eventually spent the night huddled under a boulder at the French camp; tentless, Netti and I slept in a tiny yak-herds' shelter an hour away, saved from going all day without food only by the generosity of the French; while David, choosing to go exploring on a particularly dark night, lost the path amidst a maze of yak-trails and repented at leisure on the cold hillside. Rather shamefaced and to the only partly concealed amusement of the French, we rejoined forces the following morning. Our solitary tent, when it was finally pitched, came in for some slightly superior glances, too. Apparently it was not a 'tente isothermique', whatever that may be. We were secretly pleased, therefore, despite their kindness to us, when, after an uncomfortable night above the snow-line and without reaching the col, they decided that their equipment was inadequate and beat a retreat.

In the meantime, a short second day had taken us to the snow-line at 4400 metres. The strongest porter was persuaded to stay on an extra day, proving himself a natural with axe and crampons and helping us carry heavy loads to just below the col. Thereafter we were our own porters and two more days' hard work, ferrying loads through deep snow, saw us comfortably ensconced on a rock platform the far side of the Dhampus Pass. The only intruders on our privacy were a pair of hungry ravens with a weakness for sugar. Otherwise, we were gloriously alone in a silent, empty mountain world.

The weather was excellent, apart from a bitter ever-present breeze, but unfortunately we had to cope with snow knee-deep or worse. The higher we went, the deeper the snow. Nor was it simply soft snow, for a thin crust had formed over it which became the bane of our existence. Never quite firm enough to bear one's weight for more than a step or two — and then the second person was bound to break through instead — it yet forced one to step up before it collapsed. A more exhausting surface would be hard to imagine. The wind added

117

the finishing touch to our plight by ensuring that the steps we made were quickly filled in by drifting snow. We succeeded in climbing two easy peaks on either side of the Dhampus Pass but, faced with the prospect of struggling up nearly 2000 metres under such conditions, an attempt on Tukche Peak fizzled out almost before it had started. The sun continued to shine but our enthusiasm began to wane. On ski, moving about the valley would have been both easy and enjoyable. On foot it was purgatory.

Consequently, after only a week inside the Hidden Valley and with plenty of food left, we found ourselves wondering what to do next. David was keen to stay in the valley using a tiny one-man bivouac tent but Netti and I preferred to go exploring so we agreed to split forces. Netti and I were to continue down the Hidden Valley into the Keha Lungpa valley, which would eventually bring us back to the Kali Gandaki and so to Tukche, thus completing a large circle. David decided to attempt a small but spectacular rock spire on the western rim of the Hidden Valley. In the event, discretion proved the better part of valour, and a combination of crevasses and snow conditions thwarted him when he tried to cross the ridge into a neighbouring valley system. Savouring the experience of real solitude, he made his way back in leisurely stages and rejoined us at Tukche after a week on his own.

In the meantime, Netti and I had had a more exciting and taxing time than we had bargained for. It transpires that the route we embarked upon so lightheartedly had been tried at least once before, without success. But, 'fools rush in where angels fear to tread' and we set off fully expecting to be out of the valley the same evening. Apart from indicating that a river flowed down the Hidden Valley, the contourless trekking map gave no useful information whatsoever, but even from the Dhampus Pass we had been able to see that, lower down, the valley narrowed to a gorge. We naively believed that this gorge would debouch almost immediately into the Keha Lungpa, and that it would be obvious whether or not we could pass through it.

In the first two hours, we covered less than a mile thanks to the snow, despite going steadily downhill. The river, already broad and swift-flowing, though only just released from the ice, was chuckling cheerfully on our left. Animal tracks were everywhere and we could see two herds of mountain sheep browsing on islands of rock and grass protruding from the snow. All at once, with little or no transition, the crust was thick enough to bear our weight. For the first time in two weeks we walked on a firm surface, effortlessly it seemed, and soon we were approaching the gorge.

Our pleasure was short-lived. The rock portals we had seen from the Pass proved to be no obstacle but, far from opening out into the Keha Lungpa as we had hoped, the gorge merely twisted round to the left out of sight. The sun was obviously a rare visitor, for the snow had remained powdery and unconsolidated, treacherously concealing a boulder bed over which we slid, slipped, stumbled and fell, every lurch and painful recovery made a panting effort by the altitude and the weight on our backs. Only where frozen avalanche debris had been spewed out by side gullies was the going any easier, so we were thankful to reach a point where a huge avalanche had flowed right down the gorge, completely obliterating the river Here the gorge was perhaps two hundred feet wide, its rock walls, almost vertical, towering up on either side. For several hundred yards we followed its twists and turns, scrambling over a contorted surface like a bowl of whipped meringue suddenly frozen solid. But it was firm to the foot, and we were far from grumbling. Temporarily the river re-emerged in a swirling pool, but a gangway of ice leading to a cavity behind a huge boulder, enabled us to creep between sheer rock and the water. Beyond, the river was once more smothered and we continued to pick our way round spires and over ramparts of dirty ice. The gorge was becoming narrower and narrower. As we rounded each new bend we still half expected to find ourselves entering the main valley, but with every step the fear grew that we should find the river filling the gorge and the way impassable.

Finally the ice did come to an end and the river came noisily foaming out from beneath it. The right bank was still feasible, however, and we floundered on, among snow-covered boulders again, until the cliffs dropped abruptly into the water. The left bank looked more hopeful, but first we had to cross the river. There was only one place where it looked possible. Two boulders in midstream supported growths of ice which, if they were solid, would provide stepping, or rather, jumping stones. The stream was swift and deep, however, and weighted with a heavy pack a slip could be fatal. We roped up and put on crampons and I lassoed a spike of rock upstream as a belay. Netti went first, leaving her rucksack behind. The first ice mushroom held but when she landed on the second, it slid away entire from its base. As it did so, Netti managed to topple over sideways so that she fell into the water upstream of the boulder, thus saving herself from being swept away. Regaining her feet, she made a lurching plunge for the far side and, embedding the pick of her axe into apparently solid ice, attempted to pull herself up. She was almost out when the whole slab of ice, several square feet in area, broke away from the rock beneath and she was left scraping frantically with her axe for a purchase. Luckily she found something and a few seconds later she was sprawled, gasping on the rock.

When she had recovered, she hauled the sack across and I followed, crampons scratching on the bared rocks, like fingernails down a blackboard. "This has to be the end of the gorge," I said reassuringly. "We'll camp as soon as we're out of it." Hopefully, we rounded the next corner, only to be confronted by another cliff falling straight into the water. There was no option but to recross the river. Luckily it had widened and was shallow enough to ford, but we managed to wet more than just our legs, nonetheless. Leaping across a deep channel onto a platform of rotten ice, I fell in up to the waist. The cold took my breath away. Further across, Netti lost her footing and fell on hands and knees in the water, her sack shooting over her head making it impossible to stand up again without help. Rather than plough through the soft snow on the bank, we waded now by choice along the shallows at the river edge until it became necessary to cross over yet again.

Immediately in front, the gorge narrowed to a defile a mere forty feet wide but helpfully plugged with snow. On both sides, rock walls rose compact and sheer for over 300 metres, though so foreshortened that it was difficult to judge the height. In a recess of the left wall was a huge slit similar to Ossian's Cave in Glencoe. On the bank beneath this cave was a strip of flat crusted snow, the perfect site for a tent. I pointed it out to Netti. "Let's go on a bit," she answered. "I'd much rather get out of the valley before stopping. I don't like this place at all." I knew what she meant.

Dark and enclosed, it was not a friendly spot, and we should sleep better for knowing, one way or the other, whether we were going to get through the gorge. But there was no indication that we were anywhere near the end of it, and there was only half an hour to dark. This was the first potential camp site we had come across since entering the gorge and there might not be another. Tired out and shivering violently, we set up the tent and crawled inside. As things turned out, it was just as well we did stop. But I, for one, slept badly, disturbed by troubled dreams.

Next morning, we climbed over the jumbled ice blocking the defile and scrambled along a shelf about fifty feet above the river. Then a rope became necessary. It had to be the second rope as the first, after its wetting the previous day, had frozen into a solid lump. The problem was stepping across a narrow zawn which bit deeply into the slope. Poised over it, one foot on each wall, and water seething and gurgling below, was more unnerving than difficult, but the traverse which followed, down and across a rock wall to reach the river bank again, was genuinely hard. The rock was steep conglomerate which was liable to flake away in large chunks, and I was forced to take my rucksack off to climb it. Once down, we fastened the rope at each end so that it could be used as a handrail, albeit a flexible one. When Netti had come across, I went back and forth fetching the sacks, extremely glad of the rope as the weight threatened to pull me over backwards.

Until the next bend the going was relatively easy, but far above the sun had reached the top of the cliffs and stones loosened from their casing of ice, were now humming and whining about us. Hastily we dug out helmets which, until now, had never been worn. Almost immediately a pebble bounced off my head.

Round the bend our troubles began in earnest. Here, as we had been dreading, the river completely filled the gorge. A deep, fiercely racing torrent, there could be no question of wading it; nor was there anywhere to wade to, for the far side was uncompromisingly steep and draped with ice. For fifty feet on our side there was a scoop of smooth water-polished rock, only just above the rushing water and roofed by rock a few feet overhead. Then the cliff dropped vertically into the river and as the gorge wriggled round in one of its innumerable sinuations, we could see no more. Packs off, rope on. The climbing was delicate, the rock slippery-smooth. I was very much aware that if I fell in, rope or no rope, I would not get out again — the holdless rock and the pressure of the water would see to that.

At the end of the scoop I discovered that if I could climb up twenty foot, it would be possible to continue along another horizontal fault at a higher level. Those twenty feet were hard. The start was overhanging and though the angle eased above, the difficulty did not. Precariously, I tip-toed up a holdless, snow-covered slab relying entirely on 'faith and friction' — without much of either. The traverse was on the same smooth, crackless rock as before, the roof overhead squeezing hands and feet closer and closer together until I was bent double. And then I came face to face with a vertical column of ice spilling down the rock. My heart sank. The ice jutted out like the prow of a ship completely obscuring the view so that, until we could round it, there was still no knowing whether we were going to escape from the gorge; and by this time, we really were thinking in terms of escape. But if the ice continued at the same angle — as it did on the other side of the river, great sheets of it, like washing hung up to dry — it would be unclimbable, and we should have to retrace our footsteps back up the valley. It was a prospect that did not bear thinking about.

But before I could go on, I needed crampons and the other rope. Netti was out of sight and could not possibly hear me above the roaring of water, so, tying off the rope, I climbed back the way I had come. I found Netti looking cold and anxious, still holding the rope and wondering why it had stopped moving. Hers was the unenviable task.

We shared a bar of chocolate and then I set off again, fixing the rope at several points to enable Netti to follow. When I reached the ice she was still some way behind, but, impatient to see what lay beyond, I put on my crampons, tied on to the second rope — wirelike, but at least uncoilable now — and attacked the problem. Having hacked a large step high in the ice for my right foot, I heaved on an icicle and stood up. Leaning out on the icicle as far as I dared, I peered round the ice-prow and saw, to my unspeakable relief, that it was only a small frozen watercourse and not continuous. Cautiously I changed feet and, putting my trust in the embedded pick of my ice-axe, stretched across until I could place my right foot on rock. The next few feet, across a steep rock wall blotched with ice, proved to be the hardest of all and would have been graded Very Severe at home. With only side-pulls for the fingers to keep me in balance, I progressed by carefully placing individual crampon points on tiny knobs of rock or sticking the front two 'lobster claws' into lumps of ice. Although I was tied to the rope, it could do me little good if no-one was holding it, and I was breathing heavily, not just with the altitude, by the time I reached easier ground. Thankfully, I sat down in a small cave to rest.

At last, the gorge was widening and the difficulties seemed to be almost over. Beyond the cave was another steep wall, but at the foot of it was an icy cat-walk just above the river. I drove in an ice-piton, attached the rope to it, and slid down. Leaving the rope, I picked my way downstream for fifty yards or so, cramponing up and down little walls and stepping across frothing inlets. An appropriate sting in the tail, forty foot of loose, ice-scaled rock demanding great care, and I was on top of a knoll from where I could see for certain that we were through the gorge. Ahead, it widened out into a proper valley and though I found it puzzling that there was still no sign of the Keha Lungpa, there was clearly nothing insuperable before us. Elated, I returned to tell Netti the good news.

There were still the loads to fetch, however. This was far worse than the actual climbing. Not only was it strenuous, even with the help of a rope, but if the top-heavy packs were not swaying sideways, they were jammed immovably against the rock above. I did not have the strength left to climb the overhang with a load, and had to haul it up after me. Strapping on crampons on a sloping ledge too narrow to let me take a pack off, required a balancing act worthy of Blondin. All in all, it was very unpleasant; and it had to be done twice.

On top of the knoll, Netti took her pack and carried on while I went back for mine. Dark was falling and I was near the end of my tether by the time I followed Netti's crampon marks up and across a small stream, bowed like Saint Christopher under a load that seemed to grow heavier moment by moment. I was resigning myself to a long trudge when, unexpectedly, I came across the tent snugly pitched in a grassy hollow. Netti was bending over a guy. "Somebody's had a fire here, and there's yak dung everywhere," she told me excitedly. We were back in the land of the living.

As I wearily took off boots and gaiters before they could freeze rigid, I glanced back the way we had come. Suddenly, in my mind's eye, I saw the sketch map (which was in David's possession), the river flowing out of the Hidden Valley represented by a thicker line than that flowing down the upper Keha Lungpa. It dawned on me that the apparently insignificant side-gully whose stream we had just crossed was in reality, the main valley, the Keha Lungpa, which at that point itself narrowed to little more than a gorge. The Hidden Valley was behind us and somewhere nearby there must be a path.

Our journey was far from over. Three days of hard walking with very little food, along a switch-back path often obliterated by avalanche debris still lay between us and Kagbeni in the Kali Gandaki. From there, it was to take another two days to reach Tukche. But the anxiety and suspense were at an end. Mentally, we could relax.

The gorge was a dark, forbidding gash down a mountainside of snow and scree; above it, like a streetlamp in a gloomy alleyway, hung a crescent moon, already bright in the gloaming.

"Happy?" I asked Netti. Smiling, she nodded and delved in her rucksack for a hairbrush.

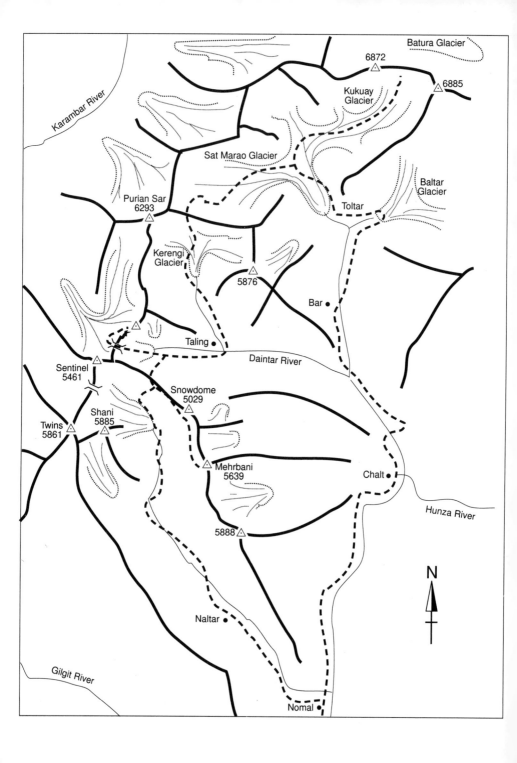

# A SUMMER IN GILGIT (1976)

Ever since we had shared a tent in the Himalaya in 1973, Dick Isherwood and I had been plotting a two-man expedition to climb in the Karakoram mountains. I use the word 'plotting' advisedly, for we would be in no way official and of planning there was little, and that hindered by the peripatetic nature of Dick's job in the Far East. One of the last communications I received was a card scribbled in an aeroplane and posted in Japan. It read: "How About Distaghil Sar? Buy a goat in Hispar and drive it up the glacier. Dick." Distaghil Sar is 7885 metres high. Investigation revealed that despite several attempts it has only been climbed once, and then after a struggle involving ice-cliffs, avalanches and violent storms. However, the Hispar Glacier is forty miles long and surrounded by peaks only slightly lower and considerably less dangerous, so I was quite content to head in that general direction.

With three kilos of potato powder and some freeze-dried meat in my rucksack to supplement the goat, I flew to Pakistan on June 21st. I was met by Dick with the news that, because of work on the Karakoram Highway, Hunza, the northernmost province of Pakistan and the only feasible approach to the Hispar Glacier, had been closed to foreigners. Following an old Himalayan trade route but built for political and military rather than commercial reasons, the 'KK Highway' runs from Islamabad to Kashgar, in Chinese Turkestan, over the 16,000 ft Kunjerab Pass (where, according to Dick who had reached it clandestinely the previous year, there is nothing save a sign reading "CHINA. DRIVE ON THE RIGHT"). Work still goes on, however, widening, metalling and endlessly repairing the road. The prohibition on foreign tourists seems to have been prompted mainly by the objection of several thousand Chinese labourers and engineers to being photographed. At all events, plans to climb around the Hispar Glacier had to be shelved.

We had other strings to our bow, but the immediate problem was to reach Gilgit. This scruffy but strategically-placed little town is the unavoidable gateway to the western Karakoram, but the road to it from the plains was also infested with Chinese and out of bounds to foreigners. With the road closed, air flights were even more heavily subscribed than usual, with a booking list stretching into August. That in itself meant little, but Rawalpindi was suffering from the vagaries of its erratic monsoon and many of the daily flights had been cancelled. Rawalpindi was full of long-faced expeditioners of many nationalities, some of whom had been waiting a fortnight already. Neither Dick nor I are good waiters and, besides, Dick had only four weeks' holiday. So, after one abortive visit to the airport, we decided to take the long way round through Swat and Chitral, small states to the south and west of Gilgit.

Two days' travel, mostly by minibus, saw us at Matiltan in Swat state, a village which boasts an unusual flyover irrigation system of hollowed-out tree trunks on stilts. Set amid fields of maize, wheat and potatoes, its solid stone-built houses are shaded by huge walnut trees and enjoy a fine view of the twin Bateen peaks. Its people, however, seemingly untouched by their environment, are grasping and unfriendly.

Our plan was to walk up the Ushu Gol (valley) and over the Kachikani An (pass) to Sor Laspur in Chitral. From there we would have to cross the Shandhur Pass, and travel down the long length of the Gilgit valley, much of which, however, can be done in a jeep. Our original concept had seen us tottering under 35 kilo loads up a glacier to a mountain. Faced with intense heat and several days' walk up and down passes, with loads which were nearer 45 kilos than 35 we admitted defeat and decided to hire two porters to help. Easier said than done.

We had both been to Swat in the Sixties, but things have changed considerably since then. We found that organised trekking, both by foreigners and Pakistanis, has become popular and as a result, wages have increased by a factor of four or five. Porters were not inclined to haggle. In Matiltan those who were found themselves set upon by a vigorous Trade Union movement, the militancy of whose members seemed to be directly related to their affluence. It was only with difficulty that we found two men, or rather a man and a boy, sufficiently impecunious to defy the militants and accept our terms.

The Ushu valley, though not without its arid sections, is a lovely place. Its stands of pine and deodar, its water meadows dotted with ponies and cattle, and the snowy peaks visible at either end, make it as picturesque as anything in the Alps. Springs of fresh water bubble up among banks of orchids. Beside the path bloom familiar flowers — cinquefoil, forget-me-not, comfrey, stitchwort, celandine, gentian, even the ubiquitous dandelion. And there are birds everywhere — beside the turbulent white glacier stream, dippers and white-capped and plumbeous redstarts; where the river has flooded, sandpipers and the striking black and yellow citrine wagtail; on open rocky hillsides, kestrels and black redstarts; and among the trees, rose finches, and cuckoos calling insistently. Dick, ever on the watch with his powerful Leitz glasses, was compiling a checklist which had soon exceeded fifty species.

The only discordant notes in this idyll were struck by our predecessors. Earlier the same month a party led by one Mr. Langlands, who I am told teaches at a school in Lahore, had travelled up the valley. We knew this because either Mr. Langlands or one of his acolytes appears to suffer acutely from the 'Kilroy was here' syndrome. At least once in every day's march the legend 'Mr. Langlands' and the date, artistically enclosed in Urdu script, would appear painted on a prominent rock. We were compelled to follow the progress of Mr. Langlands all the way up the Ushu Gol, into Chitral and even some of the way down the Gilgit valley. We wished that, like Kilroy, he could have confined his activities to lavatory walls.

Two days ahead of us from Matiltan was a commercially-organised trekking party of fifteen Americans led by a Pakistani, with a huge number of porters. Of their passage, too, we were left in no doubt, following a trail of Kodachrome boxes, sweet papers and fruit drink packets until, near the end of the second day's walk, we caught up with them, camped in a birchwood not far from the snow-line. They were so affable and welcoming, however, that I did not have the heart to give vent to my feelings.

The Kachikani An proved straightforward enough, though without a guide the correct route might not have been obvious and from the opposite direction would, I suspect, be even less so. We spent most of the day on snow. The porters were not strong and in their plastic shoes made heavy weather of the steep sections. I was no faster. A "touch of the sun" the previous day had made me feel so poorly that I had eaten and, more important, drunk virtually nothing. As a result, I was badly dehydrated and found every upward step an effort.

Another day's walk through a very different, near desert, landscape brightened only by dog roses and purple vetch, brought us to Sor Laspur — a prosperous well-irrigated village sited, like so many in these parts, on an alluvial fan. Here we had to change porters, the villagers being jealous of their territorial rights.

Finally, in a twenty-five mile day, we crossed the long plateau of the Shandhur Pass to reach Teru. In December 1895, the Pass was the scene of an epic crossing by Colonel Kelly, on his way to the relief of a beleaguered garrison in Chitral, when unfortunate sepoys from the Punjab had to drag their cannon through two metres of snow. In summer, though, cattle graze upon it and there is even a polo ground laid out. In days gone by, the annual polo match between Chitral and Gilgit, held on top of the pass in August, was the social event of the year. Alas, the advent of the jeep has made the ownership of a horse a luxury rather than a necessity, and the match is no longer played.

The sight of a blue-throat, so rare in England, only a few feet away and quite undisturbed, enlivened a dull walk on the far side. But almost as memorable for their homely associations in that foreign setting, were house martins swooping over the broad white river and, in Teru, skylarks singing above the fields. Over the last few miles, however, I noticed little. In the glare of mid-afternoon, my feet swelled and swelled until it seemed as if, like the princess in the fairy tale, I could feel the tiniest pebble through the thick rubber soles of my boots. The two porters from Laspur must have found it a long day also, for they arrived late in the evening driving their loads before them on a donkey.

A rough road runs right to the top of the Shandhur Pass but only occasionally do jeeps go even as far as Teru. We were in luck, for one arrived that night which took us sixty-odd miles down the hospitable Gilgit valley the following day, more than once being flagged down to sample the first fruits of the apricot harvest. Rather than continue to Gilgit itself, we now decided to travel up the Ishkoman valley to the Karumbar Glacier, from which we could attempt Kampire Dior.

After various vicissitudes involving jeep-drivers and bouts of a mysterious fever, we eventually reached the roadhead at Imit, renowned locally for its opium poppies. On the way, we had been given every assistance by the police in our desire to "visit the glaciers." But here we were met by a gentleman from military Intelligence who was quite emphatic that a permit was needed and that "law is law." Despondently we walked twelve miles back to the next village where we found a jeep going to Gilgit.

We spent only one night in that unprepossessing place and next day took a jeep along the spectacular mountain road to Chalt, thirty miles north of Gilgit in the Hunza Gorge (the Karakoram Highway running along the opposite bank of the river). In addition to the usual oft-described horrors of such roads, we found ourselves perched high up on top of sacks of flour and lumps of rock salt, in imminent danger of decapitation by branches, telegraph wires and overhanging rock, though in a good position to help ourselves to apricots.

Foiled twice now, we were making for two unclimbed peaks of 6800 metres at the head of the Kukuay (pronounced Cook-ooa) Glacier. Again, the local police were friendly and helpful — "you are our guests" — and as there is no frontier in the vicinity, this time there was no sign of the army. Putting our belongings on a horse, we reached Bar, the last village in the valley, in four hours and started the lengthy process of finding porters.

In Gilgit we had pared our baggage down considerably and, with only a fortnight of Dick's holiday left, we needed less food. The two loads probably weighed less than 30 kilos each and normally we would have had no hesitation in shouldering them ourselves. In fact, the following morning when negotiations broke down, we did so and we were not bluffing. Nevertheless I, for one, was relieved when, after half a mile, the porters and their representatives caught us up and agreed to our price. I was finding the searing heat and the dryness of the atmosphere very trying. (A German expedition to this region, in 1954, estimated the relative humidity to be often less than 10%.)

The porters agreed to our rate of payment but insisted on lighter loads, and by the time we had taken our own climbing sacks they were left with no more than 20 kilos apiece. With loads so light, they might have been expected to travel relatively fast. Instead, the distance we covered that first day from Bar was so paltry that we would have paid them off there and then had I not been feeling, again, the effects of dehydration.

We spent that night outside a goatherds' shelter which had clearly been occupied by the goats as well as the herds, and I put in some determined drinking. As a result, I went much better the next day. Initially, we tried to stay with the porters, but they were impervious to hints and the combination of a rest every quarter of an hour and a pace that would not have been out of keeping in a dead march, was too much for our patience. Anxious not to walk through the heat of the day unnecessarily, we went on ahead, vowing to pay the porters off that night.

Having crossed the moraine-covered snout of the Baltar glacier in a long detour enforced by an uncrossable river, and returned to the stony wastes of the main valley we reached, about midday, the place called Toltar — or what we took to be Toltar. There was nothing there but a few charred sticks and some dry stone walling beneath a boulder. But the porters had made it clear that Toltar was the day's objective, so we sat down to wait for them. (Returning that way some weeks later, I discovered that it had been, in fact, 300 metres above our heads in a narrow ablation valley whose existence we never suspected from below. However, the porters would have had to pass us to reach the exiguous path, visible only to the eye of faith, which slants up to it across a high moraine wall.)

The porters never came. Every hour or so we carefully scanned the valley with binoculars but there was never a sign of them. Dick read Richard Burton on Sindh. Having rashly left my book behind in the interests of weight, I contemplated alternately the sky and my navel. The hours passed and we began to feel hungry. Finally, as evening drew in, we unrolled our sleeping bags and tried unsuccessfully to stave off the pangs in sleep. Just before dark, Dick had a final look round but still there was nothing to be seen, not even the smoke of a fire.

Next morning our hunger was no less, but, convinced that the porters must be nearby, we left our sacks and backtracked a mile or so, searching and shouting. We were certain that they could not have passed us. Not only were we keeping a look-out, but at that point, there is so little room between the mountainside and the river that they could hardly help but see us. But there was neither sight nor sound of the two men. With nothing to eat, there was no alternative but to beat a retreat to Bar, by now a highly desirable land flowing with chapattis and salt tea.

At the insistence of the villagers, who professed themselves certain that the porters would return any moment, we spent two days in Bar, lying in the shade of a walnut tree. An almost morbid fear of the police stemmed, we learned later, from a successful raid in search of stolen property only a fortnight before. So strong was this fear that it induced the local prophet to go into a convulsive trance, wherein he was bold enough to foretell the very hour of their arrival. Unfortunately he was wrong. In the meantime, we lived on what the villagers chose to provide, mostly mulberries and chapattis of mature vintage, sometimes eggs and, on one memorable occasion, a packet of vermicelli, a tin of cheese and a large quantity of sugar boiled up together into an edible glue. However, two days seems a very long time when one is a public spectacle throughout the hours of daylight and has nothing to do but debate the likelihood of villainy or disaster. Eventually, when requests that we stay showed signs of hardening into a refusal to let us leave, we flitted on a dark moonless night to Chalt — our noiseless departure marred only by Dick's describing a somersault from one terraced field to the next, wrenching a knee in the process. In Chalt we made a statement to the Inspector of Police and, after a day over-indulging in apricots and sweet biscuits, returned to Gilgit full of gloom.

With a damaged knee and his holiday almost over, Dick cut short the fiasco of our 'expedition' by taking the first available flight back to Rawalpindi.

Within minutes of his departure, I met a policeman from Chalt in the bazaar and learned that our baggage had been recovered. Back in Chalt, I was told that the porters had brought it in themselves, claiming to have carried it all the way to the Kukuay glacier and back and demanding nine days' wages for their pains. Unfortunately the Inspector believed them. Apparently one of them had made the pilgrimage to Mecca and "They are very gentle men." Secretly, I wondered if a man who had been to Mecca might not be all the more anxious to con an infidel. Aloud, I voiced the suspicion that they might have spent most of those days reclining in the shade of a birch grove beside the Baltar Glacier, a known beauty spot. But there was no convincing the Inspector and in the end, suspecting that we might be seeing more of both the officialdom of Chalt and the men of Bar, I reluctantly handed over nine days' wages.

Before I could depart with the baggage, however, there was a formality to be observed. "Please check that everything is here," said the Inspector. He had already done so himself, using the list attached to our statement, but now it had to be done again. I was rather embarrassed as two fascinated constables, like children with a Christmas stocking, drew forth ropes, ice-axes, hammers, pitons, karabiners, crampons and high-altitude boots in quick succession. But the Inspector seemed unperturbed. Despite our insistence that we only wanted to "visit the glaciers," he was no fool and must have known better. The important thing, as far as he was concerned, was that we were not an Expedition. The ruling of the Pakistan government is that Expeditions to climb mountains must apply to Islamabad for permission, whereupon (maybe a year later ) they are charged a royalty of $1000 US, given a liaison officer whom they must fully equip and, more often than not, informed that they may climb a totally different peak to the one requested. But, as the Inspector knew from personal experience, expeditions have at least eight members and require hundreds of porters. As we patently were not an expedition, he could see no reason why we should not climb mountains if we wanted to; though why we should want to was beyond his comprehension.

Dick had gone home without setting foot on a mountain. I was more fortunate, having plenty of time and having already arranged to meet two other friends, Rob Ferguson and Dave Wilkinson, to climb in the same area. There was hope yet. I returned to Gilgit where the locals were perplexed by the mixed messages given out by my appearance. I had hair recently cropped short in the bazaar but wore loose-fitting cotton clothes, local style, and was quite comfortable eating with my hand. "Are you tourist or are you hippie?" asked one bureaucrat plaintively. I did not regard myself as either but I kept very quiet about my intentions for the next ten hot, sticky, interminable days.

Within a week of Rob and Dave's arrival we were in a position to climb something. It was not one of the Kukuay peaks but it was a mountain, and after the frustrations of the previous weeks, that was the main thing.

The auguries had seemed auspicious when, only an hour after reaching the village of Naltar by jeep, we had hired three porters and were on our way. And they were not proved wrong. Two short days of walking through a landscape of waterfalls, pine trees and flower-filled meadows, very different from anything I had seen since the Ushu Gol in Swat, took us to a height of 3800 metres. Beside the stony and chaotic Shani glacier, at the foot of grass slopes where delicious rhubarb grew in profusion and where, to our astonishment, not only goats and cattle but even some water-buffalo were grazing, we paid off the porters.

Nearby, a convenient spur ran up through pastures and steep scree to the corniced crest of a ridge separating the Naltar from the Daintar valley. Despite the usual problems associated with unfitness and acclimatization — headaches, lassitude, loss of appetite — during the next four days we transferred ourselves and our belongings to the top of the ridge, traversed perhaps a mile along it, and continued over a small peak of 5000 metres. This peak had been christened Snow Dome by an English party which attempted it in 1970 ( they were thwarted by bad weather ). The name seemed apt enough until we came to descend the Janus face of the mountain — fifteen hundred feet of black, evilly loose cliffs and scree that took far longer than the ascent.

On the col beneath, however, was a campsite that could hardly have been bettered. The tent fitted neatly onto a strip of shale — so much warmer and more comfortable than snow for camping on — beside a tiny turquoise tarn of clear melt water, twenty metres across. Here we basked in the afternoon sun, lulled by the lapping of water, letting our eyes wander over the view. To the west it was obscured by an ice-wall which served as a slight shield from the prevailing wind. But to the east one looked over green alps and wooded slopes to the brown, barren walls of the Hunza gorge and the magnificent peaks of the Western Karakoram, the massive cone of Rakaposhi dominating the whole scene in its proximity and symmetrical splendour. Above our heads was the mountain we hoped to climb, rising steeply in a series of snow slopes, arêtes and rock pinnacles to a tower which we knew to be only halfway up. From the top of Snow Dome we had had a better view of it. Only 5700 metres high, it was a midget compared with the peaks of the Hindu Kush and Hindu Raj in the distant west or the giants of the Karakoram, stretching from Kampire Dior in the north-east right round to Nanga Parbat away in the south-east. But for sheer siren elegance it could compare with any of them. In the valley it had presented a rocky west face and a steep-sided north ridge of snow broken up by rock steps. But from Snow Dome it took on quite a different character. The east face was revealed as a mass of deeply-etched flutings and snow-smothered rock, while our ridge twisted and curled away in a set of bewitchingly malevolent cornices. It was a beautiful sight, and a little daunting, too.

We left the tent at three in the morning, hoping to be high on the mountain before the sun should soften the snow. There was a waning sliver of a moon, not bright enough to dim the stars but enough to cast my shadow on the snow. Ahead, the other two were using torches, the circles of light probing leftwards for the cornice. A breeze sent particles of snow rustling across the slope and set the laces of Rob's gaiters tap-tapping against his leg, like halyards on a mast. Occasionally there was a grunt as someone broke through the crust deep into sugary powder beneath. Zigzagging up snow-slopes that steepened and eased and steepened again, faithfully following the sinuations of the ridge, we gained height steadily. With the first outcrops of broken rock the climbing became more varied. One moment we were scrambling up and down along the crest of the ridge, the next dropping below it to avoid difficulties, traversing on snow or ice whichever side was easier.

The terrain was serious — the rock loose, the snow unstable, the drops on either side, though we could not see them in the dark, huge. Yet, as with many a ridge in the Alps, to have climbed it in pitches, belaying with the rope, would have taken days. One alternative was to move together with the rope on. On a sharply defined ridge, if one man slips his companion can then save him by throwing himself down the opposite side. But the drawback to moving together on a corniced ridge is that you have to run uphill before you can throw yourself over. If this is accomplished you are liable to find yourself dangling in mid-air. If it is *not* accomplished, moving together is quite likely to prove a way of dying together. Indeed, many lives have been lost through an over-reliance on the magical properties of a rope. For the time being we preferred to climb unroped.

The sky began to lighten, Rakaposhi took on a hazy, purplish hue, and as we abseiled down some overhanging rock the sun's rays spread fan-like from behind distant peaks. Briefly, we were engulfed in a flood of gold. Then we were continuing up shaded snow slopes towards the halfway tower, the ridge crest to our left glittering in the sunlight.

The tower was by-passed on mixed rock and ice, steep enough to make us use the rope. After one pitch we moved together, keeping the rope on, for here we could protect ourselves with running belays on rock, The slope was becoming even steeper, however, and a compact rock buttress, the first of the real difficulties, lay just ahead. Hammering a piton into a crack, we belayed and began to move one at a time.

The next 200 metres were the crux of the climb. Dave, who had been discovering that load-carrying is not his forte, came into his own here and did a magnificent job. He coped with dangerously loose, wet snow with a speed and surety Rob and I would have been hard put to match; climbed equally loose rock with the same confidence; and handled with ease a long ice-pitch which would not have been out of place in one of the harder gullies on Ben Nevis. The key pitch I, for one, would not have cared to lead. The difficulty here was caused by a deep gash, four metres wide, that cut right through the mountain. It was spanned by a snow-bridge so tenuously attached at the far end that one could look through it. From this bridge it was necessary to step onto an all but vertical wall of snow overlooking the gully, roofed by icicles and, a few feet below, completely undercut. The wall had to be traversed for three metres until a lattice-work of unsupported ice served as a bridge for the last few moves onto solid rock. How the whole thing held I do not know. Even following was an unnerving experience. If any of that fragile structure had given way, having first hit the gully wall with considerable force, one would have been left hanging with little or no chance of climbing out. Dave, however, simply took it in his stride in a remarkable display of sang-froid.

Above, the difficulties eased and we could move together again, but the climb was far from over. Time had been passing all too rapidly. Although huge cumulo-nimbus clouds had obscured Rakaposhi and the other big peaks from time to time, and the occasional outrider had drifted in our direction, the sun had been beating down most of the day. Breeches had long been saturated by soggy snow and dripping icicles, and mittens had needed wringing out periodically. Now the sun was sinking. Rob was muttering about bivouac sites, but Dave and I preferred not to hear. Over two rock bumps, then an unwelcome drop and a steep climb out of the gap. More ridge, more bumps, and glimpses, looking back, of enormous cornices. At last, nothing but 100 metres of open snow slope, with some crevasses to side-step. Dave was tired, not surprisingly, and Rob was feeling the altitude. Glad to contribute after following in Dave's footsteps for so long, I went in front and trampled a trail through deep snow to the top.

The summit was a snow ridge, slightly corniced. We chopped it down and sat on the crest in a row. I do not think any of us felt particularly excited — just tired, and suddenly aware that both night and a storm were creeping up menacingly. The thunder clouds had become a uniform grey pall which had spread over us, obscuring the sun. As we watched, the pall began to drop and close in, obliterating peaks as it came. Alarmed, we descended rapidly, pursued by rumblings of thunder. For a few brief moments the sun reappeared, gilding the snow in eerie contrast to the darkness of the sky. Then it disappeared for good and the greyness was all about us.

There was a hold-up in the descent. At the back, I could not see what was causing it. Standing on the crest of the ridge, holding coils of rope, I waited impatiently. A few beads of hail fell and the surface of the snow seemed to be spluttering. My hair felt strange. Putting up a hand I found it was rising of its own accord. The air was alive with static electricity. When my axe began to hum as well, I dived for the nearest boulder — partly to avoid being the most prominent object on the ridge but chiefly, I must confess, to be out of sight of whoever sits 'up there' throwing thunderbolts.

However, we were lucky. By the time we had dug out a bivouac platform and settled into our sleeping-bags, the hail had stopped and a few stars were visible. There were one or two showers in the night, but by morning the weather was as good as ever, the big peaks having borne the brunt of the storm.

Four long abseils took us down the main difficulties, next day. By climbing straight down steep ice onto a hanging glacier, we were able to skirt much of the ridge, regaining it just before the initial snow slopes. From this point we looked down onto the brilliant splash of blue on the col and the welcoming yellow speck of the tent beside it. At the sight, the elation which had been so conspicuously absent on the summit, welled up within me. Mingling with pleasure in the beauty of our surroundings and delight at the isolation of our position, it became a conscious, exuberant happiness as I hurried on down. Being conscious, it was accompanied by gratitude — to Rob and Dave, to the weather, not least to the mountain itself. Dismissing grammatical objections, we called it Mehrbani (pronounced "Merra-bani") which, besides being suitably euphonious, in Urdu means "Thankyou".

Having climbed Mehrbani, the prospect of clambering back up the disintegrating cliffs and mobile screes of Snow Dome was as unwelcome as their descent had been unpleasant. Instead, we dropped down a small glacier and contoured long across the hillside, passing beneath a cliff where a welcome spring of fresh water spouted forth as if the rock had been struck by Moses, crossing nullahs and projecting ridges, streams and snow patches, and finally scree-running a stone-chute of a gully to reach the high pastures. Cattle tracks led comfortably round to the spur we had originally followed, a mass of gentians, forget-me-not and cranesbill making me feel that, truly, 'our days were a joy and our path through flowers'. We camped back on the crest of the ridge, where we had left a cache of food.

Next day we found an uncorniced section of ridge and, after lowering the rucksacks the first few metres, quickly descended 1200 metres of snow, scree and scrub willow to the Daintar valley, slowed only at the bottom by two tiers of continuous cliffs. There we indulged in a rest day, a luxury we could ill afford with so little time at our disposal, and we were to regret it later. It was not even particularly restful, for we were plagued by flies during the day and by inquisitive cattle, attracted by the campfire, at night. With relief, we broke camp and set off to climb the peak of 5961 metres which dominates the head of the valley.

A harmless little glacier led to a col of 4900 metres where we were able to level out a platform for the tent among some rocks, To our amazement, even here there was a trickle of melt water draining downwards. It was another perfect campsite, with a superb view down the valley to Rakaposhi and our own peak, Mehrbani. Later, we discovered that this col had been crossed by Younghusband, on his way to Ishkoman, in the eighteen nineties, but it does not seem to have been visited since.

For the climb we started early again, and after threading a hesitant way through some crevasses by torchlight, gained height quickly on the broad snowfields that comprise the south ridge of the mountain. Only near the top did the ridge narrow and become corniced, forcing us to traverse steeply in a way which brought back memories of the Lyskamm above Zermatt. The summit was a small tower of rock and snow, which gave a flourish to the end of the climb, but nowhere did we need the rope.

It was not the climbing that was memorable but the surroundings. The whole of the Hindu Raj on the one hand, and the Western Karakoram on the other, unfolded about us, acquiring first shape, and then depth, and finally colour as the day dawned and we rose higher. We sat on top for a long time, content just to gaze, and muse on what we saw. For once there were no worries about time, weather or the difficulties of the descent. Nothing mattered, except that we were alone with the rising sun in a high and beautiful place.

When we did descend, we moved rapidly and were back at the tent by ten. Continuing down the glacier, we picked up the food we had hidden among some boulders and pressed on, following well-worn goat tracks through birch groves and across moraines. On the outskirts of the village of Taling we stopped for the night, having descended nearly 3000 metres.

When Rob and Dave first arrived in Gilgit I had persuaded them that, while the 6800 metre peaks at the head of the Kukuay glacier were still worthwhile objectives, it would be more interesting to approach them from the Naltar valley. On the map the logic of this is not obvious, as they are separated by three large, and little known glacier systems, and two high ridges, only one of which had been crossed before. With little more than three weeks available to us, such a route could not but reduce our chances of climbing the Kukuay peaks; indeed, we might never reach them. But, during the long days of waiting in Gilgit, my dislike of Bar and its inhabitants had grown almost paranoic. Moreover, for many of us who climb mountains, the urge is irresistible not just to stand upon summits, but to peer round the next ridge, to cross the next col, to 'travel always a little further'. The journey, I argued, would be a mountaineering challenge in its own right probably as great as the ascent of any single peak could be — providing, at the same time, opportunities to climb smaller peaks on the way. Rob and Dave, weary from a fortnight of futile commuting to and from Rawalpindi airport and anxious only to escape into the mountains as quickly as possible, had agreed willingly enough to the change of plan. Now, having made two good climbs and reduced the amount of food to be carried on our backs, it was time to be moving if we were to have a chance of attempting one or other of the Kukuay peaks.

Taling lies at the junction of the north and south branches of the Daintar valley. Having just descended the south branch, we now followed goat tracks up the north to the Kerengi glacier, hoping to find a way across the watershed to the Sat Marao glacier, which merges with the lower Kukuay.

The Kerengi glacier bore little relation to any of the maps in our possession. Instead of a vague pear-shape we found three major branches, one swinging round to the west, the other two to the east. Formidable icefalls guarded the way up all of them, stretching in an unbroken barrier right across the valley. This was a surprise, for neither the Cambridge expedition of 1954, warming up for Rakaposhi, nor Trevor Braham in 1970, had experienced any great difficulty on their brief forays up the glacier. Acting on what we had seen from Snow Dome and Mehrbani, we front-pointed a way through at the joint of the western and central arms. There we left the glacier and toiled up 300 metres of old moraine to a small hanging glacier. At the head of a gentle snowfield lay the lowest point of the watershed ridge.

Reaching a col is always exciting — suddenly, a new world lies revealed. But it becomes doubly so when it has not been visited before. There is always a chance that the far side will prove impossible, and that, tail between legs, one will have to retrace one's footsteps. That we knew to have been the experience of Tilman at the head of the Kukuay glacier in 1947. And our first glance over this col was not reassuring. The far side was a rock wall, steep and loose, 250 metres high; the glacier below was no more welcoming, riven and fractured even before it dived away out of sight in a tangle of broken ice, littered with blocks fallen from above, and fed on either side by innumerable ice-falls, all highly active. We were so disturbed by the sight that we camped early that day, on the col, in order to recce the way down. In the event, the route we took was not particularly difficult, and only the last hundred feet required an abseil. Moreover, being on the crest of a slight spur it was protected from the stonefall of which there was ample evidence. Nevertheless, I doubt if it will ever achieve great popularity as a pass. Like Whymper's Col Dolent or Mummery's Col du Lyon it is more likely to remain simply a col which has been crossed.

Our passage down the glacier was long, complicated, at times even technical, and rendered unpleasant by steady drizzle. The weather, which had been lowering for two days, had now broken and was to remain unsettled for the rest of our time in the mountains. Once off the ice, our troubles were far from over. The best part of an afternoon was wasted in a tempting flower-filled ablation valley which petered out into cliffs, leaving us to abseil back to the glacier. And once onto the Kukuay glacier the going became truly horrible. The glacier itself was a choppy sea of ice-cored, boulder covered waves, and the slight trough between it and a steep-sided moraine offered as alternatives only pools of slush, ice concealed by mud, and a fair chance of being hit by rocks sliding off the edge of the glacier. Eventually, having crossed a tributary, we thankfully left the glacier, scaled the moraine wall, fought through a jungle of willow and birch scrub, and suddenly found ourselves in Eden.

In the ablation valley — really more a terrace than a valley — between the glacier and a mountainside of crag and scree, lay a rush-fringed lake of a delicate pale green. It was overlooked by aiguilles of rock and ice, and on its shores willow-herb and golden rod were growing gaily. Mallard took flight as we approached. Dragonflies hovered above the water. A pair of blue-throats flitted among the bushes. Happily, we pulled off boots and socks and paddled our sweating feet in the cool water. This was the place called Darrakush which Tilman had visited from Bar and which Dick and I had failed to reach. To our amazement, it was apparent that, despite the Kukuay glacier, the spot was regularly used by goatherds and their flocks. Droppings lay everywhere and the rickety roof of a crude brushwood shelter provided the only flat campsite we could find.

Here we decided to split up. Although the distance from Taling to Darrakush can be no more than twenty miles, it had taken us six days — much longer than expected, and we were running short of food. Dave, who had been suffering from an uncomfortable pack frame, kept the tent and headed down the valley towards Bar on his own. Rob and I, with the stove, bivouac sack and six days food, set off up the glacier. As there is a vertical interval of 3300 metres between Darrakush and the summit of either Kukuay peak, and a three day walk, at least, back to Bar, we had no time to spare.

To our relief, the going on the glacier gradually became easier until finally the stones gave way to ice and we could make rapid progress. The eastern of the two peaks, that on the right of Tilman's col, is a daunting spire of rock tipped with snow, which would be a magnificent but difficult climb. The western peak is more amenable, with a long snow ridge sloping down to the col. However, the ridge seemed much *too* long and we decided to reach it more directly by climbing a broad couloir-cum-ice-fall on the flank facing us. We bivouacked at the foot of it.

In the small hours of the morning it began to rain. When the clouds cleared at dawn, determined to be optimistic, we started up the snow — deep and unfrozen at first, becoming icy once clear of the lower ice-fall. We were fit and acclimatized and going well. I am confident that, barring an unforeseen and insuperable obstacle on the summit ridge, we would have reached the top that day. But it was not to be. We had climbed 400 metres and were perhaps a third of the way to the ridge, when the clouds rolled in again and it began to snow. We sat in the bivi sack for an hour drinking tea and feeling our toes grow cold, and then began the descent. There was nothing to be done but follow Dave down the valley. We simply did not have the food to wait for the weather; and, in fact, it continued to rain, off and on, for the next week. We were disappointed, naturally. But though the Kukuay peaks had originally been our main objective, the journey to them had long since become less a means than an end in itself. Disappointment there was, but no feeling of failure, or even of anti-climax — the journey was not yet over.

Having spent the night back at Darrakush, we crossed the Kukuay glacier (finding bear tracks in the sand at its edge) and picked up a path through birch woods in the ablation valley on its true left bank. Passing through two deserted goatherd settlements, one of which must be Toltar, we descended an unpleasant moraine wall, some 200 metres high, by a far from obvious path. We reached the valley bottom a hundred metres above the spot where Dick and I had waited fruitlessly for our porters, thus confirming our suspicions, for they would have had to pass us to reach Toltar. After a damp night in a cave, we caught up Dave the next day, near the Baltar glacier. He was glad to see us but even more pleased to see the stove, for his efforts at fire-lighting with sodden wood had met with scant success. The rain caused other problems. Streams which Dick and I had jumped across, now had to be waded, with a rope; nearer civilisation, paths and bridges had disappeared; and below Bar we found ourselves traversing a vertical wall of crumbling conglomerate, where once there had been a road, a few feet above swirling grey water. Nowhere, all summer, had I been so near to falling off; and nowhere, perhaps, would the consequences have been more serious.

The fields of Bar were a rich gold and full of women reaping, despite the damp. The apples were ripe, and there were still some apricots on the trees. I had begun to revise my opinion of Bar when we were discovered by a mob of unmannerly children and pursued out of the village. At Chalt we relaxed in the chai-shop — only to learn that here, too, the road had suffered and we would have to walk a further fifteen miles. Finally, we found a jeep and, in company with fifteen other passengers, not to mention suitcases, rifles, umbrellas and baskets of grapes, bumped our way inconspicuously into Gilgit.

That should have been the end of the story but it was not. Once again, seats on the aircraft were oversubscribed and many flights had been cancelled because of the weather. I had a rendezvous in Delhi a week hence and after one fruitless visit to the airport I decided it might well be quicker and would certainly be more interesting to walk than to wait. Buying a large bag of small, crisp apples and another of freshly-baked biscuits in the bazaar, I hitched a lift up the Gilgit valley as far as a landslide near Gupis. Putting my best foot forward, I walked a hundred miles or so in the next three days over the Shandhur Pass and down into Chitral. Finally, I was picked up by a Polish engineer in a jeep and given a ride the rest of the way to Chitral town. The following day I shared the price of a jeep with a French couple I had met. Easily the most hair-raising moments of the entire trip were on the precipitous descent of the Lawowri Pass in a thunderstorm, in a vehicle with faulty windscreen wipers, and bald tyres that slithered about on the slick dirt surface of innumerable hairpins. The French couple shouted and screamed incessantly but the driver, high as a kite on hashish, merely laughed manically and steered one-handed as he turned round to gesticulate to his passengers with the other. Three days later I was in Delhi, to discover that somewhere along the way I had picked up head-lice.

# The Quality of the Experience

# ONLY A HILL (1987)

Only a hill: earth set a little higher
Above the face of the earth: a larger view
Of little fields and roads: a little nigher
To clouds and silence: what is that to you?
Only a hill; but all of life to me ...
*Geoffrey Winthrop Young*

Behind my home in Eastern Snowdonia lies an unexceptional little hill. Only 600 metres high, it is not worthy of the serious hillwalker's attention. To east and west drain glaciated valleys filled with unlovely conifers, one of them doomed to become a reservoir sooner or later. To the north is a rough region of heather and innumerable hillocks, dells, and little crags, all recently planted over by the Forestry Commission. To the south, a moor of mat and tussock grass and bog cotton stretches to the derelict quarries of Blaenau Ffestiniog. There is a Bronze Age cairn on the summit, and several hut circles and long houses have disappeared beneath trees in the cwm below, but the area as a whole has been described by Pete Crew as "an archaeological Desert". The rocks are acid, so there are no unusual arctic-alpines to be found on the small crags beneath the summit: and although peregrines and black grouse breed not far away, and crossbills and red squirrels are to be found in the forest, it is not renowned for its wildlife. As I said, it is an unexceptional hill.

Yet for me it is special. From its summit can be seen virtually every mountain group in Snowdonia; there is a great spaciousness up there; and, above all, it is quiet, with the quietness of a place rarely visited. Once, years ago, I met Iorwerth Lewis out on the moor, checking his sheep on horseback as he used to in Patagonia. I have gone up there with Nedw Pritchard to mend fences. But in all the dozens, maybe hundreds of times I have walked or run over that piece of Wales, I have never met another walker. True, the sheep-path that used to veer to one side of the summit has grown a little more defined and now runs straight to it. Once or twice recently I have found pop cans and sandwich packets stuffed between the stones of the cairn. There is no doubt that others, besides myself, know this place. But it is not much frequented. More than anywhere else in the world I have valued that empty mountain top, for if to the Welsh culture of the valley I will always be an outsider, up there I am at home, there I can go at any time, at any season, and be received unconditionally, as by a parent.

Landscape can never be static. Change is implicit in the processes of growth and decay, evolution and erosion. The swiftest changes, however, if one excepts the occasional catastrophe, are usually man-made and for the worse, even in National Parks. Eight years ago an agricultural road was built from Dolwyddelan to the top edge of the forest, at the 400 metre contour on the northern slopes of the mountain. Two years ago the JCB was at work again, extending the road further up the hillside. Then, for over a year, nothing happened. All one winter, the JCB lay abandoned on the hill, visible from afar like some prehistoric roosting bird, seemingly impotent. The new 'road' was an impassable quagmire and it seemed as though the withdrawal of EEC grants had called a halt to proceedings. Alas, it was not to be. This August, I heard rumours that the roadhead was snaking its way still further up the hill. Running home from Capel Curig one day, I decided to investigate. The road was now well packed and drained and obviously in use, and as it rose higher and higher up the hillside my consternation grew. As if to rub salt in the wound, I heard an engine behind me. On ground where I had never met a soul before, I was passed by a car containing four passengers, with a hang-glider on the roof. On and on, inexorably, unbelievably, wound the road to end finally on the very crest of the ridge, only three hundred yards from the summit, in a turning circle where the car was parked.

I could have wept. Inwardly, I did. For that hill-top will never be quite the same again, at least, not in our lifetime. The mere existence of that track, crudely hacked out of the hillside, has destroyed the feel of the place. The views will be the same, but the experience of seeing those views will have insensibly altered, for beauty is an experience in people, not a quality in things. As Ansel Adams wrote of telegraph wires visible from footpaths in the Yosemite National Park: 'They are little things it is true, but they signify a very important thing. They break the vital thread of perfection; they destroy the mood which, after all, is the most precious factor in the relation of man to nature'.

Moreover, that summit will no longer be unfrequented. The road will be seen as a boon by the organizers of Arduous Training, Duke of Edinburgh expeditions and Unaccompanied Walks from centres. "Elitist!" goes up the familiar howl. But is it not sufficient that the highest and finest mountain in England and Wales can be reached by train; that Glaslyn can be reached by vehicle track; that the Devil's Kitchen can be reached by not one but two paths of motorway proportions; that the Carneddau can be penetrated by tarmac road to Ffynnon Llugwy in the south or by Landrover track to the summit of Drum in the north; and that countless forestry roads had already made access shorter and easier to most of the smaller hills of Snowdonia, even before the latest wave of agricultural 'improvement'.

I cannot blame Mr. Williams for building that road. If offered something for nothing: which of us would refuse? An EEC grant of 80% paid on a fixed cost basis, has meant that many farmers have built themselves roads for nothing at all, and not a few have made a fat profit. It is another example of the inappropriate application of the CAP, the wasteful use of public funds, and the helplessness of a National Park authority which until last November had literally no control over what farmers did on or with their land. It is all very well to subsidise sheep farming to maintain a traditional way of life, but to destroy the landscape of a National Park in order to alter and mechanize that way of life is an absurd irony. Admittedly, things have changed. EEC grants for roads have been cut to 30%, and farm buildings and roads are now subject to planning constraints — albeit eligible for compensation if permission is refused. But for many parts of upland Britain, it is too late. All over Snowdonia, mile upon mile of ugly bulldozed tracks, of derisory agricultural benefit, traverse what were the most genuinely wild parts of the Park.

I am not sure why I am writing this. It cannot unmake that road. I am crying over spilled milk. It does not even make me feel better. My initial rage has given way to a sort of despair at the eczema creeping over the face of the land. What were symbols of freedom for body and spirit are now ever-shrinking pockets of land enclosed by wire, roads and signposts. The landscape's vitality has been diminished, what we can feel and experience there cheapened. I am reminded of the passage in Jacquetta Hawkes' marvellous book *A Land*, where she describes what has happened to Stonehenge:

'If its incorporation in a great work of art — book, poem or painting — can immensely heighten the quality and significance of some natural or artificial feature so also it can be debased by man. Cafes and chewing gum, car parks

145

and conducted excursions, a sense of the hackneyed induced by postcards, calendars and cheap guidebooks has done more to damage Stonehenge than the plundering of some of its stones. It will never again be possible to see it as Constable did when he made his studies, a place of mystery against a background of storms and flying showers; it is doubtful if it could ever again have the deep impact on any man that it once had on Wordsworth; it seems no longer a setting fit for one of Hardy's gigantic, stereoscopic scenes. Men made it and men have destroyed it, the whole action taking place in the realm of the imagination.'

Men did not make my hill, but they have as surely destroyed its spirit and mood as they have the spirit and mystery our ancestors celebrated at Stonehenge. Where does the process lead, and where does it end?

Postscript: Since writing this the JCB has returned. Despite, or even because of a remonstrance to the National Park Authority, a toothless tiger if ever there was one, the road has now been gouged to the very summit, an act of deliberate vandalism, I suspect.

# ADVENTURE VERSUS THE MOUNTAIN (1984)

As an Outdoor Pursuits instructor, first at Ogwen Cottage, latterly at Plas y Brenin, I have, for some years, vehemently defended myself against the charge that I, and others like me, are filling our tiny but precious mountains with youngsters who do not want to be there, and gain nothing by being there. Now I am beginning to have my doubts. It is a rare teenager who really enjoys the river as well as the rapid, the mountain as well as the climb. It is action, thrills, adventure that matter most, rightly so at that age; and these, we are being shown, can be provided as effectively in the city as in the hills; initially, at any rate.

A taste for landscape, for natural beauty, for wildness (as opposed to wilderness, which we do not have) is not innate in human beings, it seems; it is an educated response. It is a truism that mountains were usually feared and disliked, occasionally venerated, but certainly not enjoyed until the eighteenth century. The writings first of Rousseau, then of the Lakeland poets, of Ruskin, Thoreau and Jefferies, changed all that, but it is no coincidence that the early climbers were from the educated middle-class, often academics. It was not just a question of leisure and cash, it was the way they had learnt to look at mountains in an age of proliferating man-made ugliness. Today, the Romantic view of mountains permeates the pages of Climber and Mountain, but it is an educated attitude nonetheless, one that has been acquired through experience, talking and reading. The silence, the space, the solitude so valued by many, though admittedly not all, adult mountaineers, may be actually threatening to a youngster impelled into it from the heart of a city. He reacts by yelling raucously into an empty cwm, shattering with stones the mirror of an upland lake, and throwing aside his crisp packet and empty pop-can. Not only is there none of that 'sense of wonder, that most precious of gifts, the birthright of every child' that Shipton believed in, but for any other who had entered that cwm, like R S Thomas, 'on soft foot, breath held like a cap in the hand', the moment is destroyed and the place sullied.

Why a sense of wonder is so noticeably absent in inner-city groups, I do not know. It could be a total lack of familiarity with fields and woods, let alone mountains; or excessive exposure to the vicarious experience of television; or a protective shell grown against the innumerable hurts and failures of school. Maybe, as teenagers, they are just too grown-up and worldly-wise. I do not know. But repeated disappointment at the reaction of groups to the mountain ambience has led me to revise my attitude towards outdoor education. It is not so much a conviction that our approach has been wrong all along, as that it has become inappropriate. Things have changed since the outdoor pursuits boom of twenty years ago. On the one hand, government agencies like the CEGB, the Welsh Water Authority and the Forestry Commission, for all their glib assurances, have continued inexorably to build, plant and disfigure the landscape, and with their persistent demand for service roads to whittle away the remoteness and effective scale of our mountains; while the jets and helicopters of the armed forces all too often render the 'peace of the hills' a hollow myth. On the other hand, the numbers of climbers, walkers and canoeists enjoying the mountains has multiplied staggeringly. This can only be a good thing, vindicating the existence of our National Parks. But these pressures combined create a situation in which we can no longer afford to bring youngsters into the mountains unless they actively want to be there. Otherwise we will destroy completely the qualities for which we value mountains. We will kill the goose that lays the golden egg.

Yet the last three or four years has seen the growth of yet another source of pressure, a fresh invasion of the mountains. I am referring to YOP courses and the like. A good idea in themselves, they have been the salvation of many a struggling centre and the making of many an entrepreneur, so criticism is unlikely to be popular. But many youngsters attend only grudgingly, because otherwise they would not be paid, and the prime purpose of such courses is to provide a residential experience, which could be obtained effectively almost anywhere away from home. The educational benefit to largely unappreciative youngsters does not justify the environmental damage to our National Parks and other wild places. In Snowdonia, the litter on summits has, if anything, decreased, but, through the clear waters of every lake, tin cans glitter and broken glass makes bathing hazardous. High campsites are betrayed from afar by rings of stones; closer inspection reveals a wider circle of blue Marvel sachets and poly bags, and in all probability a pile of rubbish shoved under a boulder. Even underground, in old mine workings, a powerful sense of recent history is diminished by a trail of sweet papers and torch batteries. Still, long crocodiles of bright orange anoraks and clusters of orange tents destroy the delicate but important illusion that the landscape is empty, or nearly so. And the impact of many an outdoor experience, be it on a mountain top or crag, or in a gorge or mine, is reduced by overcrowding as local centres and, increasingly, inner city groups, flock to the same venues. Some blame must be attached to leaders and instructors. But, really, the situation has been brought about by bringing youngsters, often against their will, to places that they care nothing for.

There is no doubt that for many an unemployed school-leaver, the only prospect for positive living lies in a hobby or sport, and the potential of outdoor activities here is enormous. But expensive residentials are not the most effective way to spark off an enthusiasm, let alone sustain it. Rather than use the mountains as an outdoor gymnasium as we do at present, outdoor pursuits, adventure activities, call them what you will, should start in the city where they will cost relatively little, can involve greater numbers than heretofore, and can allow for continuity, progression and involvement with a project. Those who enjoy this introduction can progress to activities, with or without the acquiring of skills, in the 'urban fringe', the countryside accessible from the city. A visit to Snowdonia, or the Lakes, could be something of a climax to a period of training for those who have become hooked on a particular sport, or on the outdoors in general. It does not automatically follow, but often an awareness of the natural world develops alongside the acquisition of skills and a broadening of experience. Therein lies my hope, both for the mountains and for the youngsters concerned.

Instead of the one-off introductory courses that are their bread and butter, LEA centres would play a more useful role providing advanced courses for groups, not necessarily from schools, who already have the basic skills and really want to be there. Less than 1% of Birmingham's schoolchildren ever visit Ogwen Cottage. Most of that 1% enjoy themselves, but only a very small proportion appreciate the mountain setting and the personal and social development that undoubtedly does take place, even in a week, could equally well occur nearer home. Terry Nicholls has been making this point for a long time and putting his ideas into practice in Sunderland. Others are now doing the same in London, Manchester, Nottingham, Liverpool, Birmingham, Edinburgh, and no doubt many other places. The Community Leaders' courses, instigated by Roger Orgill, which we have been running at Plas y Brenin for the last four years, must have added impetus to this movement, though being in the heart of Snowdonia they have always been anomalous, and would seem to be no longer necessary.

Such an approach is not elitist. It makes both the excitement and the multifaceted education of outdoor pursuits available to far greater numbers yet makes it more likely that our fragile and dwindling inheritance of wild country is used by those who value it and treat it with respect. I am not suggesting that mountains be preserved for the privileged middle class or for a mountaineering elite. On the contrary, I see them being more heavily used than ever. What I *am* suggesting is that we try to bring youngsters to the hills who are already on the way to being canoeists, climbers or hill-walkers, and confine introductory adventure education to the neighbourhood of school or home, which is not, in fact, a great limitation. Wild and beautiful places are important for the well-being of our society: that is the raison d'être for our National Parks. My concern is for the inner city as much as for the mountain. What we are doing at the moment is of negligible benefit to the one and disastrous for the other.

# BEAUTIFUL BRITISH COLUMBIA (1990)

STOP TREE ROT — BUGGER A HUGGER. The words blared out in strident yellow paint from a bridge near Tofino on the west coast of Vancouver Island. We were approaching an environmental front-line where feelings run high on both sides and protesters have not been afraid to step over the legal line into civil disobedience. Conflict between loggers, for whom trees are simply timber to be cut down, and environmentalists, who are prepared to hug a tree to keep the chain-saws at bay, has become endemic in British Columbia — Beautiful British Columbia as the registration plate of every vehicle proclaims.

For over a hundred years the logging companies have had carte blanche to cut down whatever they like, and have done so in a staggeringly profligate way. When an area is clear cut it is routine for 50% and sometimes as much as 80% of the felled trees to be abandoned as less than perfect. Forests have been regarded as a resource to be plundered rather than carefully husbanded. Although theoretically all felled areas should have been replanted, this has only happened on a small scale and in the more public areas, until very recently. The forestry companies preferred to leave regeneration to nature on the assumption that there would always be more virgin forest to cut into; and government officials seemed happy to turn a blind eye to the fact.

Now, there is a massive replanting scheme underway — 3 billion seedlings a year the Forestry Service claims — but it will be many years before there are new forests or, rather, plantations, to harvest on the scale the logging companies are used to. In the meanwhile they are resorting to heli-logging inaccessible areas and developing ways of using aspen and cotton-wood, formerly regarded as weeds. But the main effort is still to mop up what areas of virgin timber remain.

Forestry is big business in British Columbia. Undeniably, it provides a lot of jobs and is the province's most profitable export. Nobody disputes the importance of timber in the provincial economy. It is the destructive manner in which logging is carried out and the lack of long-term planning that are causing conflict. The logging companies form an extremely powerful lobby which spends 8-10 million dollars a year ensuring that its political presence is felt. Even bigger

151

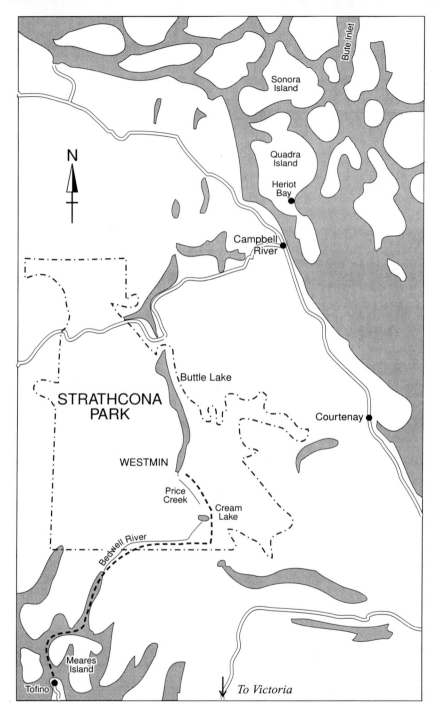

The area shown is part of Vancouver Island and lies NW of Vancouver City.
This map also refers to the article "West Coast Wilderness" on p179.

sums are spent on publicity campaigns like the primetime TV advertisement which insists that 'Forests are Forever'. Over the last few years, logging companies have been combining into a few giant cartels. The largest of these are themselves subsidiaries of multi-national corporations not noted for their environmental concern. Recently, for the first time, these companies have been meeting a resistance so vocal and so effective in eliciting public support that the provincial government has been forced to listen. The resistance comes from an alliance of environmentalists, who value wilderness for itself and as a spiritual resource; Indians, for whom areas like Meare's Island and the Stein valley are traditional sacred sites; and other local residents who see the future lying as much with tourism as with logging, fishing or mining. In the case of Meare's Island, the campaign was based on the little town of Tofino and after a protracted struggle lasting years the island was saved.

As we chugged across Clayoquot Sound in the elderly M.V. Superstud, piloted by Johnny Tom, a local Indian, we were travelling in the same direction as the environmental running battle. For the activists of Tofino the centre of attention has now shifted northwards to Sulphur Passage. The Friends of Clayoquot Sound are campaigning for 'sustainable development' of the last big tract of virgin rain-forest left in the region. With the backing of the Tofino Chamber of Commerce and a high proportion of local residents, they would like to see selective logging, preserving certain areas, taking only prime timber out of others so that the forest remains a community of different species at different stages of growth rather than the sterile plantations which are all too familiar in Britain. Clear felling, where permitted, should be in small blocks at a time to reduce visual impact and erosion, with careful replanting afterwards. They argue that clear-cutting will not only replace a beautiful wilderness with a hideously scarred landscape that takes years to recover, even partially, and will certainly not be a tourist attraction, but also causes soil erosion and landsliding which will endanger the spawning grounds of salmon and affect fish farms out in the Sound. What the Friends of Clayoquot Sound are proposing is a multiple-use plan for the area which will be in the long-term interests of all its inhabitants.

The logging company concerned are not interested. Selective logging is less profitable than clear-cutting and they are accustomed to a Tree Farm License giving them all the rights (but none of the responsibilities) of ownership. The two biggest companies made a clear profit of 500 million dollars in 1987. One cannot help suspecting that their intransigence stems more from a reluctance to be held accountable than from concern over a loss in revenue. It is easier to feel sympathy for the individual logger who fears that his livelihood and way of life may be at stake.

When we stepped off the bow of the Superstud onto a rocky shore at the head of Bedwell Inlet, and the throb of the engine died away, we realised with something of a shock that we were now totally on our own. True, this was not pristine rain-forest. The valley was logged twenty-five years ago and the tree-cover is mostly alder and aspen. But it is a remote area from which there is no easy escape and no means of contacting the outside world. Our only way out was through the mountains by a route much of which was untracked and an unknown quantity.

Over the next four days we worked our way up the Bedwell river and across the southern portion of Strathcona Provincial Park to Buttle Lake. At first we followed the old logging road, overgrown but still easier going than the scrub on either side. Squidgy, purple droppings full of berry pips were everywhere, but we never actually saw a bear. When the road petered out we climbed 800 metres up a rocky gully to escape a fearsome tangle of devil's club thorn, thimbleberry and slide alder, a plant so flattened by snow that its stems grow parallel to a slope, instead of upward. "This is meant to be a hike," I told myself more than once, as I edged gingerly across the top of a waterfall, a 30 metre drop below, trusting to handfuls of heather or blueberry twigs, or balanced precariously up a steep slope of hard-packed conglomerate. Twice we had to use the rope to protect a rock pitch. I had been reluctant to take a rope, but my brother-in-law John knew better. At the top, we emerged into the alpine zone, a region of streams and waterfalls and little lakes in rocky hollows, in one of which John swam before breakfast while I shivered and was content to take photographs. And there were flowers everywhere, meadows bright with colour even in late September, when we had expected none : blue of lupins and homely harebell, yellow of hawkweed, monkey flower and sedum, purple and orange asters, red and yellow Indian Paintbrush, and many others. Once, we found ourselves breaking all the rules, wandering about a glacier without ice-axes. Another time, descending onto an ice-field unmarked on the map, we had to resort to a 'classic' abseil. I discovered that maps in B.C. do not bother to distinguish cliffs from terrain that is, anyway, predominately rock. Even the most widely-spaced contours may conceal unsuspected steps and bluffs, and anything that looks steep on the map is likely to be impassable without technical climbing gear. This felt like exploratory mountaineering more than walking, with all the enjoyable uncertainty and slight tension that goes with it.

Finally, we arrived at Cream Lake, a beautiful turquoise tarn, one of the jewels of Strathcona Park which was to have been drained and dammed to provide hydro-electricity for a new open-cast mine. The Friends of Strathcona have made a path up Price Creek to the lake in a successful attempt to make people aware of what was to be taken from them. But it is still a five-hour walk from the roadhead, and the path and a proliferation of fireplaces along the way is a small price to pay for saving the lake and its surroundings. We had not intended to travel out that way, but wind and rain shredded John's second-hand poncho into a clammy scarf about his neck and forced us down from Green Lake at the head of the creek. After wading crotch deep along swollen side-streams in preference to hideous alder thickets and wind-throw, we were happy to take the easy way out, squelching down through magnificent stands of giant hemlock.

We knew we were returning to civilisation when we saw the sharp zigzags of a logging road slashed across a clear-cut hillside and soon afterwards heard the humming of extractor fans at Westmin mine, several miles away. Situated in the middle of the Park yet currently employing 750 people, this mine epitomizes the shabby treatment that has been meted out to Strathcona over the years. Originally established in 1911, the Park now covers an area of 230,000 hectares of forests, lakes and glaciated mountains. Unfortunately, being a provincial rather than a national park, it has been possible for provincial governments to change its status at will without reference to the legislature. The history of the Park is a long, sad story of government-sanctioned depredation for logging, mining and hydro-electricity. Recently, yet another Order in Council arbitrarily altered the status of several sections of the Park to that of Recreational Area, a euphemism that permits logging and mining. This time the government bit off more than it could chew. Environmentalists were more organised in mobilizing support, setting up a campaign of civil disobedience that despite sixty-four arrests, successfully prevented exploratory drilling. Moreover, residents of Campbell River township were deeply disturbed at the effect further mining might have on their drinking water. Buttle Lake, twice dammed and enlarged despite protest, is already polluted with heavy metals that have leached out from mine tailings. Taken aback by the furore, the government appointed a commission to report on the future of Strathcona Park. To the astonishment of government and environmentalists alike, the commission came out wholeheartedly in favour of preserving the integrity of the Park from all further exploitation, making some trenchant criticisms of past policy in the process.

155

The government accepted the gist of the report and Cream Lake has been reprieved — in the context of the Park's history, a remarkable triumph.

Our five day journey through this wild and beautiful area made me aware how much we owe to groups like the Friends of Clayoquot Sound and the Friends of Strathcona. Regarded as pests by those whose only motive is profit, and vilified as cranks and hippies in smear campaigns, it is they and others like them who are ensuring that British Columbia remains Beautiful.

Visiting Vancouver Island again last summer it was clear that the environmental battle is far from over, and climbing in the Coast Range brought home to me how little virgin forest there is left to save. The directors of the multi-nationals in their plate-glass offices in far-away cities neither know nor care about anything other than short-term gain. But the times they are a-changing. The headline in the local paper the day I arrived read 'Loggers refuse to cut forest of 300 year old trees'. When the men who wield the chain saws start to become concerned, there is reason to hope.

# SMALL EXPEDITIONS IN THE HIMALAYA (1980)

Ever since climbers first began to visit the Himalaya at the end of the last century there have been large expeditions and small ones. Mummery, invited to join Conway's lavish investigation of the Karakoram, preferred to go to Nanga Parbat with Hastings and Collie and a couple of Gurkhas. While the Workmans and the Duke of the Abruzzi were invading the Karakoram with their miniature armies, Dr. A M Kellas was making some remarkable journeys of exploration in Sikkim and climbing peaks up to 7000 metres with only a few local porters for company. Between the wars there was a sharp contrast between the series of heavyweight expeditions to Everest, Kanchenjunga and Nanga Parbat, and the explorations of Shipton and Tilman or the success of Spencer Chapman on Chomolhari. During the so-called golden age of the fifties and early sixties when the majority of big Himalayan peaks were being climbed, most expeditions were large, for nationalism, was more blatantly and internationally rife than ever it had been on the Eigerwand and the Grandes Jorasses. But there were notable exceptions — the Austrians on Cho Oyu and Broad Peak, the British on the Muztagh Tower and the American four-man attempt on Everest.

The last fifteen years have seen Everest firmly established as an international status symbol, permanently booked up five years in advance. Not only Everest but all Nepal's 8000 metre peaks have been repeated time and time again, confounding Longstaff's hope that once Everest had been climbed mountaineers would forget about mere height and "turn to the true enjoyment of the Himalayas, most likely to be found at 20,000 feet or less". More recently, the re-opening of the Karakoram by Pakistan has sent a fresh series of massive caravans winding up the Baltoro. At the other end of the scale, there have been the groups of two, three or four climbers posing as tourists in an effort to evade increasing restrictions, regulations and expense, unobtrusively penetrating the remotest corners of the Himalaya and making many fine first ascents among the lower peaks. Initially most of these small expeditions were Austrian or Japanese, but numbers of British climbers have begun to follow suit. This trend must have been strengthened by articles by Dennis Gray, Trevor Braham and Joe Tasker which have appeared over the last few years, arguing basically that large expeditions are anachronistic. Dennis Gray in 1971 was describing the 'approach and style of application' of the first ascents of Annapurna and Everest as being 'as relative to this day as the stage coach to jet travel'. He went on to comment that "to the discerning, success means nothing, only the way it has been achieved matters". In Britain, at any rate, a climate of opinion seems to have been created in which small expeditions are regarded as desirable, whether it be from the standpoint of personal satisfaction, the health of climbing as a sport or the ecology of the Himalaya. And yet large expeditions remain the norm in Himalayan climbing. Cast an eye down the long list of expeditions that every year visit the Karakoram and Nepal and you will find that the vast majority have at least 8 members, supported by Sherpas or high-altitude porters, employ over 100 porters to reach their Base Camp and cost many thousands of pounds. Clearly, whatever the pundits say about small expeditions, climbers internationally are not convinced. Why should this be so?

I have to plead ignorance of the mechanics of organising a large expedition and hope I will be forgiven if I am simplifying, but there seem to be certain discernible strands of logic influencing the initial conception. One is the need for publicity as an aid to raising funds. Despite the startling achievements of Reinhold Messner, it is still highly unlikely that the media would give the same publicity, before the event at any rate, to a small expedition as it would to a large one, whatever its objective, so organisers tend to think in grandiose terms from the start.

A side-effect of publicity is the survival of nationalism in mountaineering, a fact to which the Nepalese Rules for Expeditions bear witness. The rules stipulate that the Liaison Officer should be equipped with a Nepalese flag to be planted on the summit alongside the national flag of the expedition. The officials of the Ministry of Tourism were genuinely puzzled that our two-man expedition to Annapurna II should neither have nor want a flag of its own. "But *all* expeditions have a flag," one of them remarked plaintively. Few expeditions nowadays are totally financed and organised on a national basis. But the requirements of the media are such that any expedition with a sufficiently formidable objective — and this can mean high rather than hard — and, above all, big enough to gain credibility, will soon become a national event, "invested," as Shipton complained years ago, "with a glamour foreign to the fundamental simplicity of the game". Climbers become national figures and under strong pressure to succeed, if only because they know they have an audience; and success is interpreted in the same distasteful manner as an Olympic gold medal.

The principle that size inspires confidence is as true in the attracting of financial sponsors as it is in the apparently necessary preliminaries of winning over the media. The team must be large, equipment the best, the budget enormous, or the men of business will not be impressed. Heavy commitment to a particular sponsor, or a film or book contract dependent on success, can exert a pressure similar to that of national expectations. And should there have been little publicity beforehand, the sponsor or sponsors will soon rectify the situation.

But whether it is financial obligation, an armchair audience or personal ambition of a not strictly mountaineering nature that is the original motivating force behind the size of a big expedition or, most likely, a blend of all three, success becomes all important and no expense is spared to ensure it. Lavish plans become yet more lavish. To eliminate the possibility of human weakness and to enable the climbers to conserve their energy for the summit, Sherpas are employed to do the hard, and often the most dangerous, work (ferrying loads through the Khumbu ice-fall into the Western Cwm, for instance). All these people, both climbers and Sherpas, have to be fed, clothed and tented, and maybe supplied with oxygen as well to make assurance doubly sure, which means the endless carrying of a vast amount of food and equipment up the mountain — most of it catering for the carriers. Ropes must be fixed to make this process easier and safer and camps must be close together for the Sherpas to get there and back in a day. (Many modern Sherpas — and this is a reflection not on them but on their employers — are much more at home with a pair of jumars than with an ice-axe.) Finally, each camp must be connected by radio so that the whole gigantic operation can be efficiently directed from below (and, on the recent French expedition to Everest, so that the climbers could speak to their wives in Paris). All this costs an awful lot of money. The only element in success which cannot be bought is the weather and this, alas, is often the decisive one.

On some expeditions of this type an unconscious belief that there is safety in numbers seems to lull climbers into a false sense of security which influences their assessment of objective dangers. This could be one reason for the frighteningly high accident rate on the big peaks. Certainly, that sense of physical isolation, commitment, self-reliance, call it what you will, which is at once so disturbing and so exhilarating and which, if pressed, I would say is what mountaineering is all about, must be virtually nil until the summit bid. In this context, it is interesting to note Chris Bonington's comments on the climbing of Brammah I (6400 metres) in Kishtwar with Nick Estcourt: "It had been a mountain holiday rather than an expedition and yet the climbing, without fixed rope and with a long summit push had, in some ways, been more committing than what we had experienced on Everest the previous autumn."

The preconceptions, then, of journalists and captains of industry go a long way towards preserving that elephantine anachronism, the large expedition; and their support, once elicited, is interpreted in terms of more men, more equipment, more money. Another factor tending to make expeditions bigger than they need be is the expense involved in gaining permission to climb. To a large expedition, the money involved is a bagatelle, but to an otherwise modest venture it can be crippling. In Nepal, for instance, you pay a peak fee of £500. Then you must fully equip a liaison officer. He will not go above Base Camp (in fact, of the three LOs with whom I have had dealings, a Pakistani, an Indian and a Nepali, not one has even got that far), but he must be equipped as well as the climbers and everything must be new. There are plenty of Sherpas in Kathmandu to tell him if he has not been given the very best — "Aha! Only a Redline. We had those in the Ice-fall." — and they will probably buy the gear off him afterwards. To add insult to injury, he must be paid over and above his police salary (and at a higher rate), and insured. For the average Nepali sub-inspector it is like a cricketer or footballer being given a benefit match, and he is determined to make the most of it. Moreover, the LO cannot be left on his own at Base Camp, if he reaches it, so the expedition must employ a cook who also must be paid, equipped and insured. And because the LO's main function is to send weekly reports to the Tourist Ministry, there has to be a mail runner as well.

By the time these extra mouths have been fed and extra porters hired to carry their food and belongings, the expedition has been compelled to spend nearly £1500 for its peak and the doubtful benefit of an LO to organise its transport and porters. For a small expedition this could well be over half its total budget. The situation is very similar in Pakistan, though not so bad in India where the peak fee is lower and the LO is expected to return his gear. For a small expedition the temptation NOT to seek official permission can be well-nigh irresistible. One alternative is simply to increase the number of climbers so as to share the expense, on the assumption that they already own the necessary equipment; but many organisers are tempted into the vicious circle of publicity, sponsorship and even greater expense to ensure success.

A final factor making for large expeditions is lack of confidence. There are three essential attributes for a Himalayan climber: alpine experience, a strong

160

stomach and the ability to acclimatize. The last is difficult to predict — many a fine climber has failed in the Himalaya on this count — though how you feel on top of Mont Blanc is, in most cases, a fair indication of how you will react higher up. The need for a strong stomach is not so bizarre as it may seem. Our excessively hygienic attitude towards food in the West leaves many of us unduly susceptible to any different forms of bacteria, not necessarily virulent ones. Yet to avoid all local food and drink is to take a lot of meaning out of the journey to and from the mountain which, for all but the most myopic, is as important a part of an expedition as the climb. General Bruce wrote, "One point to which I must again draw attention, and which is the most important of all for the explorer of the Himalaya and especially for the mountaineer — that is to have a really dependable digestion ..." Finally, experience of alpine or other glaciated mountains is of far more value than great technical skill, which will rarely be needed. Anyone who has the physical fitness and the mental approach — in particular the refusal to be intimidated by appearances or scale (which is not the same as ignoring objective dangers) — to climb a *grande course* can attempt a Himalayan peak with a reasonable chance of success. But the Himalaya are now so accessible and have been described and photographed so alluringly that, not unnaturally, many people wish to climb there who do not possess these attributes. Lacking confidence in their own ability, or perhaps worried by the hazards of illness and altitude, they take refuge in numbers and the support (sometimes, indeed, the leadership) of Sherpas.

And so the large expedition still exists and, in all probability, will continue to do so. Like Concorde, it will remain of immense importance to those involved, arousing admiration in the ignorant and indignation in the concerned. To me, it seems that the amount of money spent on the largest expeditions — £100,000 is not an unusually high figure — is shameful and quite unjustifiable. To argue that it is but a fraction of a big company's advertising budget or that far more is spent on football is beside the point when such a sum is not necessary to climb any mountain, however high or difficult.

Returning to small expeditions, confusion reigns over what exactly the term means. Nowadays nearly every expedition from Britain pays lip-service to the ideal — even the recent K2 expedition was described as 'small' which, relative to other K2 expeditions, it may have been — yet some are clearly smaller than others. And is size gauged by numbers or expense, or both? It is possible for a six-man expedition to cost half as much as a two-man expedition with a more ambitious objective or more extravagant notions.

161

I wish to put forward a definition of a small expedition as one in which all equipment and food can be carried on its members' backs in a single load. Indeed, a provocative demon urges me to go further, to put my head on the block, and declare that *all* Himalayan expeditions should conform to this criterion. Such an approach to big mountains would mean that certain problems would have to wait until there were men and materials capable of overcoming them. But is that any different from saying that a rock-climb should be left for the man able to climb it free?

I would not insist that the expedition carry everything itself on the approach march, only that it should be able to do so if, for instance, the porters went on strike. Few of us from cold climates can cope at once with the fierce heat of the foothills, and it is difficult to appreciate the flora, fauna and culture of the country through which you pass with a huge load on your back. It could be argued that, by the same token, it is not possible to enjoy climbing a mountain with a load on your back and it is, therefore, only sensible to employ Sherpas to do it. I would reply that climbing — of any sort — is only partly to do with conscious pleasure and enjoyment and much more to do with those fleeting but highly-prized moments which, for the sake of argument, I shall call happiness:

"The moment of happiness — not the sense of well-being,

Fruition, fulfilment, security or affection,

Or even a very good dinner, but the sudden illumination ..."

Probably few of us have experienced quite the sort of revelation Eliot is talking about, but many would agree that on a climb where mind and muscle are being, or have just been, taxed to the utmost, what they feel goes far beyond enjoyment, even if it is difficult to put into words and never lasts for long.

In the valleys the expedition can live off the land, saving its own food for higher up. This in itself will limit the number of climbers, for few Himalayan villages have the resources to feed large groups. Once the last village is left behind, the porters must be paid off, for now the expedition is living off its own fat (literally, no doubt, as well as metaphorically) and it will have to move faster than most porters are prepared to do. I have found it feasible to pack everything needed for three weeks in the mountains, with alpine-style mixed climbing in mind, into a 75lb load. This is most easily done with a party of three crammed into a lightweight two-man tent, as the cooking and climbing gear is no greater than it would be for two. There are plenty of other ways of saving weight. If I know it is all going on my own back, I personally carry no spare clothing except a pair of socks, and I am not convinced that a duvet jacket is necessary below 8000 metres. Several pounds can be saved by eschewing reflex cameras and additional lenses; and transistor radios, cassette tape recorders and the other means by which we insulate ourselves from our surroundings, are out of the question. Fuel can be saved by relying more on wood and dried dung, always available up to 3650 metres and often much higher, than on gaz or paraffin.

It is worth remembering Tilman's advice that "on any expedition, even the most serious, the tendency to take two of everything, just to be on the safe side, needs to be firmly suppressed". Tilman's words were endorsed by Lionel Terray, writing of the Alps just after the war when "both food and equipment were very much heavier than they are now, but above all we were weighed down by traditions as old as mountaineering itself. People always carried a little more food and gear than they really needed, just in case". With the carefully designed pack-frames now on the market, it ought to be possible for climbers of average physique but sufficient determination to carry loads of 90lb or more up to, say, 4000 metres. With greater care in the selection of food and equipment and a more drastic pruning of luxuries, it might well be possible for an expedition to be self-contained for five or six weeks. Admittedly, this would still impose severe restrictions on the ascent of a peak like K2 at the far end of the Baltoro glacier. But the effort would be worth making even there, for the right people; and for lesser mortals (myself definitely included!) there are plenty of easier and more accessible peaks in the Himalaya.

Load-carrying is enjoyable only in a masochistic sense but as with so many things, the reward is in proportion to the effort expended. For anyone who loves mountains and hates crowds, the satisfaction of travelling through wild, empty glaciated country, pitching a solitary tent every night in a new place and, perhaps as the climax but not the end of the journey, reaching a summit, must surely be self-evident. Had Shipton and Tilman been able to exchange their Meade tents, Bergen rucksacks and sacks of flour and rice for the lightweight food and equipment now available, that is how they would have been climbing. "The unattainable ideal to be kept in mind," wrote Tilman of the 1938 Everest expedition, "is two or three men carrying their food with them as in the Alps." The unattainable is now, I believe, attainable. I know it to be a perfectly feasible approach to small peaks up to 6500 metres and I can see no valid reason why it should not be applied to almost any peak; though I would echo Bruce's remark that "the true enjoyment of the Himalaya ... is to be found in the lesser ranges". It is also a very cheap way of climbing. By turning a blind eye to officialdom, it is still possible to organise a three-man trip to the Himalaya for £1000 including air travel.

Granted, with less time at your disposal you are at the mercy of the weather and the chances of failure are high; but on the other hand, if you are not establishing camps and fixing ropes, a short spell of good weather will suffice to climb most peaks, as Messner has demonstrated several times. Without the compelling need to succeed that bedevils the large expedition, many climbers will admit defeat more easily than they would be allowed to if they were part of a team; but if survival is regarded as more important than success, this is not necessarily a bad thing.

And if you do fail, what of it? The personal rewards will have been great even if public acclaim is lacking. Mountaineering is, after all, a sport, not a war, however much the language of the press may try to persuade us otherwise. Because the World Cup and the Olympic Games display so many of the characteristics of war, perhaps that is all the more reason for mountaineers to avoid a similar confusion of ends and means. In the literature of the world, mountains have traditionally been sources of inspiration, symbols of aspiration to a better life and a refuge from the values of the market-place. The early mountaineers seem to have been aware that they inherited this tradition and trod softly over the mountains they loved. Today, not only businessmen in search of a quick profit but climbers like ourselves are trampling on them, dragging the market-place lock, stock and barrel into the hills, even into the Himalaya, right up to the summit of Everest.

# TRENCH WARFARE ON MAKALU (1993)

The lower Makalu Base Camp at the head of the lovely Barun valley must be one of the most beautiful places on earth. It is situated on a flat, grassy shelf, bright with flowers, just above the stony outwash plain of the Barun glacier. The site seems totally safe but it is encircled by rock walls, noisy hanging séracs and fluted ice. Nearest and most dramatic of all is the formidable South face of Makalu itself. An inspiring place to spend a couple of months, you might think; yet for me it was not so. On the contrary, it was a profoundly depressing experience.

Disillusion set in the day we arrived at Base Camp. Initial euphoria turned to disgust as we noticed tin cans everywhere and discovered scraps of polythene and silver foil, bits of rag and old torch batteries under every boulder. Cans were scattered all over the outwash plain, blown by the wind over an area a mile long by half a mile wide. A huge open pit was full to the brim with rubbish. The so-called Hillary Base Camp was the same. So was Advanced Base, used that year by Spanish, Catalan, American and German expeditions as their Base Camp. Garbage from Britain, Poland, Japan, France, Italy, Germany and Spain was clearly recognisable — the price paid by Makalu for being an international status symbol. Almost every spot that could be camped on looked and often smelled like a municipal tip. Two of us followed the route of a trekking party up to the Sherpani La. It was easy to follow — a paper chase of luxury items imported from France. The overnight camp was a miniature version of Base Camp. No attempt had been made to burn, bury or conceal the rubbish, let alone carry it out. Higher up, every drink stop was waymarked with packets of fruit crystals and isotonic drinks, or chocolate-bar wrappers, dropped where they had been opened, in or beside the infrequent melt streams.

Up on the snow, Camps 1 and 2 were surrounded by this year's contribution: gas cylinders, foil packets, Kodachrome boxes simply tossed out of the tents, even when there were large crevasses nearby. Camp 3, above the Makalu La, was kept clear by the good offices of the wind which removed everything to deposit it who knows where. Whatever the motives that bring mountaineers to these high mountains, pleasure in pristine, unsullied landscape is clearly not one of them.

And what of ourselves? It is easy to become 'holier than thou' about these things. More than one neat bag full of rubbish and good intentions was discovered and broadcast by the ravens. There was British rubbish left behind at Advanced Base and more at Camp 1. Down in the valley we held long debates and agonised over the Base Camp mess — our own and the great communal pit below us. Should we carry everything out? If so, where to? Was it more acceptable to dump it in a Nepalese village than up in the mountains? What about dropping it in a mountain lake or in the Arun river? If it was not removed, should it be buried or was it better to leave it in an open pit to encourage others to use it? We reached no definite conclusions and in our leaderless, anarchic, British way made only individual, impromptu decisions about it. But we did collect many basketfuls of rubbish and we left the place cleaner than we found it. A dozen porterloads of old tins were sent down the valley, although when last seen they were still stacked behind the house of our assistant Sirdar. The rest we buried by filling in the pit.

A problem common to all expeditions in Nepal is that the Sherpas regard it as unlucky to burn anything until they leave a camp. Stacked behind a boulder, much of our paper and cardboard migrated down to the outwash plain, to mingle with edelweiss and blue poppy as soon as the wind blew. We had transported our food and equipment in a mixture of plastic barrels and tin trunks. The barrels were highly prized as baksheesh and were saleable items. The tin trunks, on the other hand, must have been diabolically uncomfortable to carry and once they had been battered and bashed were of little use to anyone. In the end, we left behind at least 20, on the understanding that the local yak herder would collect them in the spring to build himself a new shelter ...

Litter was not the only thing to mar my enjoyment. A hundred years ago and more, Leslie Stephen described the Alps as 'the playground of Europe'. Today, the Alps are more like a fairground and Nepal has the dubious distinction of being the new playground. Climbers from all over the world flock to its prestigious 8000 metre peaks and to the cheaper and more accessible, if misleadingly named, trekking peaks. Some of the fine peaks in between are quiet by comparison. Makalu has become so popular a goal that it now sports a guidebook in German. Hand in hand with the guidebook mentality, not only cairns but blobs of green paint mark the route up the moraine-covered glacier to Advanced Base — a piece of idiocy if ever there was one; glaciers do not move at a conveniently uniform rate and the paint marks are already more of a hindrance than a help. But then, like so many aspects of behaviour in our society, the markers were painted for the short-term benefit of one small group, with no thought for others or for the future. This is not just conservationist whingeing. At the root of any global problem you care to think of lies the inability of both governments and individuals to consider consequences, to think of other people or other species, to look to the future.

Nepal is suffering drastically from deforestation, largely as a result of population growth; but in the upper valleys climbers and trekkers have undoubtedly played their part. The Barun valley is one of the few well-wooded areas left in Nepal — but for how long? Ministry of Tourism regulations are explicit that live wood must not be cut to provide fuel for base camps and that all rubbish must be taken out. Yet, almost every day, porters laden with firewood would pass through on their way to the higher base camps. Here, at least, we had a clear conscience.

Down on the outwash plain below us, a French expedition pitched its tents. I found it sad to be woken in the morning by a generator providing the power for a satellite dish, so that a journalist could telephone daily reports to Paris. I was glad that, although we had film-makers with us, we were not under that sort of pressure to succeed; we were climbers climbing for ourselves, not gladiators performing in a public arena.

Up on the mountain, tents and fixed ropes were expendable. Once established, it seemed there was never any intention of removing them. Only the Americans and ourselves seemed particularly concerned about how the mountain was treated. And we, too, abandoned a tent. There is a school of thought, I know, that regards leaving camps as totally reasonable as they either disappear or become fair game for the next party. A variation on this attitude is that, in the total scheme of things, both ourselves and our litter are so infinitesimal that it is a waste of energy worrying about them. I cannot agree with either view. After all, we live in the here and now and react to what we see. Beauty in mountains is akin to mood. It is a personal, subjective response — an emotion in individuals rather than an objective, concrete reality. It is easily damaged, even destroyed. For me, on Makalu, it was certainly badly bruised. An incomparable mountainscape was being diminished, and the quality of what we could feel and experience there cheapened. Not everyone saw it that way, to be sure. Many seemed unaware of the tawdriness we had introduced. Was I being over sensitive? Some will think so, I know. Or was it just that being alone, or in a small group, in a genuinely wild, untrammelled landscape, and responding to it heart and soul, is an experience harder and harder to come by in this age of packaged and, all too often, irresponsible adventure? If you have never experienced unsullied 'wilderness', maybe you will suffer no pangs when you visit Makalu Base Camp; but you will also have missed out on a most precious gift. It is like a guided tour of some great mediaeval cathedral, with postcards to buy and a cream tea afterwards, compared with the worship of a fervent congregation, or kneeling there alone at dusk.

For me, it was a new experience to be on a Himalayan mountain with five other teams, not to mention a party on Baruntse and innumerable trekking groups. In some ways it was fun — a bit like climbing in Chamonix. We all made good friends with climbers of other nationalities. The downside was that Calvin Torrans had a barrel of personal possessions stolen from base camp and I had a rope and an ice-axe stolen from Camp 1. After we had decided not to go for the south-west ridge, with its infamous descent into the Cwm of Despair, and had switched our attention to the ordinary route, the Catalans suddenly became very uptight. It transpired that they resented breaking trail endlessly through deep monsoon snow and fixing ropes in a couple of places, only for others, like ourselves, to take advantage of them. It was at this point that Calvin suggested that 'trench warfare' would be an apt description of the climbing and a good title for an article. My thanks (or apologies) to him. Relations improved again after we started to do our share of trench-making. In retrospect, the most enjoyable part of the trip for me was the few days Pete Getzels and I spent mountaineering and acclimatising in perfect solitude on the big high plateau between Sherpani La and West Col.

It was a novelty, too, to be a member of such a large team and to know no one well beforehand. I enjoyed making new friends, and meals in the big mess tent made out of tarpaulins were a time for wide-ranging conversation and some good laughs. We were a diverse group of 16, a big expedition by any standards. There were ten climbers with one doubling as a doctor, four film-makers involved in two separate films, a nutritionist who monitored our body fat with a pair of giant pincers and weighed every plateful of food, a nanny, and baby Rachel, aged two and a half, who was easily the most cheerful and resilient member of the team.

Unfortunately, throughout the three months we were in Nepal, there was an underlying tension between some of the climbers and one of the film crews. What surprised me was that some very experienced, otherwise sensible people made no attempt to conceal or contain their antagonism for the duration of the trip. In terms of human relations, to my mind just as important as the climbing outcome, the trip was a disaster. The effort required on an expedition is not just physical.

I suppose another factor in my mixed feelings about the expedition was the time away from home and loved ones. Three months is a long time. But big mountains need a lot of time — for bureaucratic hassles, for a long walk in, for thorough acclimatisation and for repeated attempts. Moreover, big peaks are undeniably dangerous and it does not help when wife and children are well aware of it. Perhaps high-altitude mountaineering should be a single person's indulgence. At all events, at the back of my personal urgent desire to climb Makalu was a sense of guilt and the knowledge that it was highly unlikely that I would ever again bring myself to be so wittingly selfish.

We did not get up the mountain. The unsettled weather of the monsoon ended with a two-metre dump of snow and almost immediately the jet-stream winds of winter set in, converting all that snow to wind-slab. The 'window' of fine weather we had been waiting for never materialised. At Base Camp, we enjoyed blue skies and warm sunshine throughout October. Above the Makalu La, temperatures were in the minus 30s, the wind blew persistently at 60-70mph and the snow became steadily more dangerous. I did my best, have never tried harder, despite reaching only 7600 metres. I might have been more successful, personally, if I had had an established climbing partner from the start, as everyone else did. I learned that two days' rest after a big effort at altitude is not nearly enough. We might all have been more successful if we had recognised that, under prevailing conditions and on a non-technical route, it was more sensible to work together as a team rather than in ones and twos. But we never really had a chance of reaching the summit.

No-one that season climbed the north-west ridge of Makalu, though there were nearly fifty people trying to. The only successful ascent was of the south face by Pierre Beghin, solo. My admiration for this feat is not whole-hearted. Beghin works in an avalanche institute; he knows the effect of strong winds on powder snow. He was in radio contact with the Spaniards at Camp 3, above the Makalu La, before and during his climb. Yet when his friends decided to turn back, he chose to go on, fully aware that he would have to descend the other side of the mountain loaded with wind-slab. In the event, he was avalanched twice, surviving falls of 200 and 400 metres. No one can dispute his skill, daring and fortitude. But would he, I wonder, have climbed the south face if that journalist had not been sitting beside the telephone at Base Camp, desperate for copy to send back to a French nation celebrating the 200th anniversary of the Revolution?

When *Mountain* magazine, wrote that 'The Makalu Massif was the place to be last summer', it may have been true for Beghin, it may even have been

169

true for Steve Sustad and Victor Saunders, who, in bad weather, climbed a fine line on the west face of Makalu II and made it back down by the skin of their teeth; but it was not true for everybody.

I will be accused of sour grapes, no doubt. Had I climbed the mountain I might feel a little better about the expedition as a whole. But only a little. My experience on Makalu makes me seriously wonder whether Ruskin was right all those years ago. Perhaps all that climbers really need *is* a greased pole (or an indoor wall?). I have always assumed that, under even the most macho exterior, deep down all climbers cared for rocks and mountains, for wild places and beautiful landscapes. Why else would they climb? In Britain, self-inflicted wounds such as Craig y Forwen, where climbers have been banned because of their anti-social behaviour, made me wonder. But those were caused by irresponsible young rock-jocks, weren't they? Mountaineers are different, surely. I suppose the state of every summit in the Alps gives the lie to that one. But still I had faith. Not any more, alas.

I don't know what the solution is. Probably there isn't one. But I will not be going back to the really big mountains. A 7000 metre peak with a small group of mates — perhaps some of the friends made this time? Yes, I hope so. But an eight-thousander ... never again.

# *Wilderness Ways*

---

# HOMEWARD BOUND (1973)

Among the icebergs, clustered like browsing elephants off the northern shore of Horseshoe Island, the latest snowfall had drifted thickly, insulating a layer of melt-slush. So, although it was cold and clear, and we had rattled down Bourgeois Fjord and into Square Bay on bare wind-scoured sea-ice, like polished black cobblestones, now the surface became soggy and the going slow. Thirty yards in front of me, Malcolm's sturdy frame began to show signs of effort as his sledge and skis gouged four dark wetly glistening tram-lines out of the white. My dogs, the Picts, hated it. More concerned with avoiding the puddles than with dragging the loaded Nansen, they stopped often, turning reproachfully to inquire how long we were going to persist in such foolishness. Momentum lost, a violent shove became necessary to 'break out' the sledge — not a simple manoeuvre on skis. Nor were skis making it any easier to walk, sticking in the glutinous sludge rather than gliding. The dogs began to stop more frequently. There was nothing for it. Strapping the skis on top of the load and resigning myself to wet feet, I put my head down and pushed.

Thankfully, we emerged at last from the bergs and saw close ahead the seemingly insignificant little hump of Reluctant Island. As its name implies, it is only separated from Horseshoe Island by a matter of yards; but the coast of Horseshoe is steep, mostly ice-cliff, and offers no campsites.

In summer Reluctant Island is a favourite basking place of Weddell and Crabeater seals, and the dogs, detecting the scent, at once began to burrow down excitedly through the snow until they were scooping up shingle. In an area where violent katabatic winds of 100 mph or more can blow out miles of apparently solid sea-ice overnight, it was reassuring to know there was terra firma beneath us.

Picketing the dogs and sledges was more of a problem than usual. The snow was too soft, and the gravel too loose, to give a safe anchorage, and it was necessary to hunt around for a boss of hard ice that would take an ice-piton, or a drift of snow deep enough for a 'dead man' belay.

After setting up the pyramid tent on its four aluminium legs and placing boxes of food and jerry-cans of fuel along the valances, Malcolm disappeared inside with the groundsheet. I could hear him busily blowing up lilos. A hardy

Scot, he was the ideal travelling companion, capable and self-reliant, yet even-tempered and understanding. I was 'outside man' for the evening. I tightened the tent guys, ran out the radio aerial, collected ice-chips for water, and finally fed the dogs. The single Nutrican block was the big event of their day, for which they had been waiting expectantly ever since we halted. As soon as I approached the 'Nutty Box', a frenzied barking and howling ripped the still air. I ran between the traces, hastily throwing the greasy blocks to right and left, before the pickets could be pulled up and a bloody battle ensue.

Soon all was quiet again. By this time it should have been dark. It was only a fortnight since six of us, cut off from base by the unfrozen sea, had celebrated mid-winter in the snug little refuge on Blaiklock Island. We were only two degrees inside the Antarctic Circle, but the sun was not yet due to reappear and a gloomy daylight lasted only five hours. Tonight, however, the moon had already risen, a day past the full. The scene seemed scarcely less light than before, and infinitely more beautiful in its cold brilliance. Upon the shimmering surface of Square Bay and on the Forbes and McMorrin Glaciers, the moon shone fully, but on the mountain masses of Centre and Broken Islands and on the steep scarp wall of the Grahamland Plateau behind, prosaic gullies and ridges had been transformed into mysterious facets of black and silver. There was not a sound. Even the air was still, as if frozen like the sea. The dogs were tired and had curled up nose to tail, following me with their eyes. Our isolation was complete. Yet it brought no sense of loneliness. Sledging with dogs, whatever other emotions you may experience — and they range from love and admiration to fury and despair — you are never lonely.

It was cold, very cold. All to the good, if the sea was to freeze further out in Marguerite Bay. Tomorrow would show whether enough ice had formed to allow our return to Stonington. It was three and a half months since we had left base, and we were looking forward to some home comforts. Inside the tent, Malcolm had lit the Tilley lamp and his hunched shadow moved upon the warm pink canvas as he made tea. I was ready for it, yet reluctant to break the spell. For weeks previously we had been living with cloudy skies and wind incessantly beat the tent and blew blinding drift in our faces. Nights like this were rare and to be savoured. I longed to grasp the moment and somehow keep it for ever in a way words and celluloid never can. I shivered, and sighing just a little, crawled into the tent.

We were away early next morning. The moon had sunk and we broke camp by the light of a Tilley lamp whose brilliant glow caused the blackness to

173

close in like a threatening crowd. The dogs were shadowy forms, stretching and shaking the snow out of their coats, and beyond them was impenetrable outer darkness. But while we were busy scraping ice from the runners and harnessing the dogs, day came, and by the time I gave the command "Up dogs, Huit!," smoky pinks and yellows were creeping up the sky behind the mountains.

All went well at first. The surface was better, the dogs were pulling enthusiastically, and as I led the way out of Square Bay towards the open sea, Morag, only recently promoted leader, responded obediently to commands to move right or left. The first setback occurred when we reached new ice. Here the sea had frozen since the last snowfall and for a moment we mistook the smooth black surface, coloured by the depths beneath, for open water. I chopped a hole in the surface until water gushed up. The ice was a good six inches thick, quite safe enough to sledge on, and as it was free of snow, we looked forward to some fast travelling. We were soon disillusioned. The ice was like a pane of glass, without wrinkle or blemish. Once moving, skis and sledge continued to glide indefinitely — indeed, it was impossible to stop — but the dogs could gain no purchase at all. When they tried to pull, all four legs shot from under them and, bewildered, they sprawled painfully on their bellies. Before long, mutiny was in the air, and when finally I gave the order to swing back onto the old ice, the team turned as one. There was nothing for it but to follow the old ice towards the coast and hope that conditions might improve.

Sure enough, before long we came to a surface of solidly frozen floes on which we could once more travel seaward. Not far ahead was the rocky headland of Camp Point, a well-known landmark which we should have to round before heading south for Stonington. Beyond it, we should be sledging across a wide bay with no safe camp site for twenty miles — and if the surface was bad, twenty miles could be a very long way.

Immediately in front I could see a lead of black water splitting the ice. It looked narrow though, and the dogs had become used to jumping leads and tide-cracks in the last few weeks, so I was not unduly worried. Unfortunately, this time new and still fragile ice had formed at the edges of a fairly wide crack, leaving a deceptively narrow strip of water in the middle. Morag was some sixty feet in front of me, so I only realised this as she reached the lead. Even then, I did not realise how weak that new ice was, and urged the dogs on. As they crossed, they broke through it, rapidly widening the crack until Bran and Kon, the last pair, were swimming. It was only the pull from the rest of the team that enabled them to scramble out on the far side, powerful 100lb dogs though they were. The team was now on one side of a six foot gap and the sledge and myself on the other. Unable to think of any dry way out of the situation, I finally yelled to the team and attempted to drive across. The jerk pulled the front of the sledge onto the far side but, predictably enough, the rear sank and I, still on skis, sank with it. Not noticing that both skis had dropped off, I heaved myself out, baggy windproof trousers bulging with water, and seizing the bamboo 'cow-catcher' helped the dogs haul the sledge clear. Though my skis had vanished, vital equipment such as sleeping bags and the radio had deliberately been placed at the front so there was no serious damage done. Malcolm was soon with me, having made a detour round the lead and I decided to continue to Camp Point before changing into dry clothes, since we had been asked to check an old food depot, in any case.

In retrospect, that lead should have been a warning. The surface still seemed firm enough. Investigation revealed that the floes were a foot thick, and the frozen 'cement' binding them together at least six inches. It was the structure of the ice that proved treacherous. As I rounded Camp Point, looking for a suitable place to go ashore, I suddenly felt a floe sink beneath me. I was running beside the sledge to keep warm and before I could react, a raft of ice had tilted beneath my feet and I found myself once again immersed in icy water. Close to land, pressure from the sea beneath had become too much for the gigantic crazy-paving on which we were travelling. The floes had been forced apart and the 'cement' had reverted to a semi-frozen mush. The only hope was to keep the sledge moving, but now the dogs began to fall between the floes. As they panicked and ceased to pull, the sledge lost way until eventually it too slid sideways off a floe and began to settle into the thin skin that was covering the sea.

The situation seemed critical. Expecting the sledge to sink at any minute, I quickly cut the main-trace and unclipped the dogs from their side traces before they drowned. To my surprise, however, the sledge, though well and truly embedded, did not sink completely. Hope dawned that it could yet be saved. Attaching a rope to the 'cow-catcher', I crawled from floe to floe, making my way towards the shore twenty metres away. After several fresh duckings, I discovered that I was safe enough on the larger floes so long as I did not try to stand up. Landing was difficult since the last floe, heaving on a slight swell, was separated from a sloping bank of smooth slippery ice by a metre of water. The floe was small and the bank steep, so if I fell in I should be unable to climb out again. Taking no chances, I leaned cautiously over the gap and cut hand and foot holds with an ice-axe before delicately transferring myself to the shore. In front was a ten-foot wall of vertical ice which demanded more step cutting. Then, teeth chattering and toes numb, I set out to look for Malcolm.

Seeing my plight in time, he had returned to the far side of the headland. Now I found him in a position little better than my own, forty yards out, among loose floes, with the rear of his sledge half under water. Fortunately, his dogs had not broken through and before long, our combined efforts had heaved the sledge safely onto dry land. My feet needed immediate attention, but they soon came back to life in the warmth of Malc's sleeping bag and, without wasting any more time, we scrambled back over the broken rocks of the Point. I had been fearing the worst, but the sledge was just as I had left it, and the Picts, for once too frightened to fight, had remained huddled anxiously together on a large floe; all, that is, except Chinook, a large, cheerful, but relatively timid dog, who appeared to have been sent to Coventry and sat in splendid isolation on a small floe of his own. The first task was to clip them all back onto the main trace — not easy in the confined space of an ice-floe, with eight dogs trying to lick me and express their pleasure at my return. That done, I fastened a rope to Morag at the front of the trace, and with Malcolm pulling on the other end, they ran ashore with surprisingly little difficulty, hauling each other out of the water as they fell in. There was not room for them to stay on the shelf so each dog had to be heaved up the ice-wall and dropped down the far side; and now the fights started. It was quite some time before the team was finally spanned in the steep-walled gully beyond and the snow was liberally sprinkled with blood. That left the sledge to be rescued. I unloaded it, on hands and knees, while Malcolm hauled tent, boxes and sledge-bags ashore with the rope. At last, aided by a pulley system, the lightened sledge could be tipped onto a floe and righted. By the time we could think of pitching the tent it had long been dark and the temperature was well down in the minus twenties. I had been in wet clothes for seven hours. Shaking from cold and exposure, I wriggled thankfully into my sleeping bag, only to experience excruciating pain as the frozen tissue of fingers, toes and knees thawed out. Codeine had negligible effect and I slept very little that night.

By the following morning, each kneecap was an enormous blister, and fingers and toes were in a similar state. After contacting Stonington on the radio for medical advice, I stayed in the tent bathing the frostbite blisters in a biscuit-tin of warm water and carefully bandaging them. Meanwhile Malcolm laboured like Hercules, trudging back and forth over the 100 metres of rocky defile that separated our respective landings. Box by box he carried my 600lb load across to where his sledge was beached, moved the dogs two at a time and, finding the ice once more firmly frozen, pushed my sledge round the outside of the Point. It became apparent that the floes were only loosened by the pressure of high tide, and froze firmly together at low tide. Camp Point is potentially a highly dangerous place since, should the ice blow out, the way inland is barred by vertical rock; in effect, it is a trap. Climbing part way up the cliffs, Malc could see that the ice was unbroken right across the bay to the south, and so we decided to push on immediately before the weather broke.

By the time we were away, it was a superb moonlit night, crystal clear, with sparks of cold fire being struck from the snow and no sound but the occasional eerie creak of an imprisoned berg. It was bitterly cold. To save the blisters, I had to stand on the back of the sledge rather than ski or run. The surface was a good one so the extra weight did not affect the dogs; but they were mystified by my frenzied contortions as I flung my arms about to keep warm.

After a while I gave up the unequal struggle and sank into a frozen dream-state, on which the passing coastline and consciousness of the cold only occasionally impinged. Malcolm led the way and, with another team to follow, my dogs gave no trouble. It was with a start that I noticed a light straight ahead. We had passed the great rock prow on the far side of the Bay without my noticing it and were now only six miles from home. A Tilley lamp had been left out to guide us round the snout of a glacier which flows past Stonington's back door into the sea.

Suddenly, a dog appeared, racing round the sledge and trying to play with Morag. I assumed he must have escaped from base. It was a beautiful, almost ghostly sight, this mystery beast gambolling in the moonlight. Only when the team became so distracted that I tried to catch the stranger, did I discover that it was Jamie. Somehow he had slipped his harness, and with the hood of my anorak drawn so tight that I was peering myopically through a screen of fur, I had failed to recognise him as one of my own dogs.

Cold and tired, we reached Stonington at 5.30 in the morning. Friendly hands were waiting to unharness the dogs and picket the sledges. The interior of the hut was bright and warm and a pot of tea had been brewed. It was good to be back.

By midday the sky was overcast and the wind rising. The 'blow' lasted eight days and at the end of it every scrap of sea-ice between Stonington and Camp Point had disappeared. We had been just in time.

# WANGANUI RIVER

A splatter of wings on water,
ducks drag into the air;
from a bell-bird, skulking in the Bush,
droplets of pure sound fall
loudly, heavily, like the drips
from our paddles upon
the pewter surface. Otherwise,
silence hangs over this
glittering reach of river and
the fern-green gorge that contains it.

Blades lift and pull in unison,
minds, like water, deepen,
quieten to the rhythmic swing,
until movement without
becomes stillness within, and we are,
just for a moment, one,
and we are not on the river
but we are the river.

1988

# WEST COAST WILDERNESS (1995)

The bear — a black one we were relieved to note, not a grizzly, but a powerful, loose–limbed animal nonetheless – was about two hundred yards away, near the crest of the ridge. He paused to watch us for a moment, then continued foraging among some blueberry bushes. Fall is a good time for bears; food is plentiful and generally they are tolerant of human intruders. However, we were taking no chances and gave him a wide berth as we picked our way across white granite slabs onto the crest of the ridge. It was a beautiful place. To north, east and south glaciated mountains stretched away endlessly. Before us a deep blue lake occupied a hollow in the rock. Where water seeped out of the ground grew the creamy white flowers of Fringed Grass of Parnassus. The summit looked no distance at all, but in reality it was still two hours away.

We had woken to a temperature inversion, a sea of cloud filling the valley below cutting us off totally from the rest of the world. Our only concerns all day were elemental ones like heat, thirst, weary legs and the security of hand or foothold. Our senses were alert to the whistle of a marmot, the acrobatics of ravens, the flavour of pure spring water, and the bite of granite crystals into our fingertips. From the summit, we peered down onto the bare ice of a small decaying glacier and watched, far off, a hot air balloon being used to extract timber from the forest. We ate salmon sandwiches and home–made cookies and were startled by a bald eagle which appeared from nowhere, floating past noiselessly.

It was a long day. By the time we returned to the cabin, our faces were glowing from sun and wind, and we were more than ready for Laurie's salmon bake and apple crumble. We slept soundly that night.

* * * * *

Beneath me, the coarse granite is cushioned by a fur of dry moss and a little overlap in the rock slab creates a perfect back rest. As I write, I am reclining in this natural 'chaise longue', gazing past scattered trees – yellow cedar and western hemlock – over denser forest to the wrinkled waters of the inlet some thousands of feet below. Beyond lie the forested slopes of Sonora Island and the distant 'blue remembered hills' of Vancouver Island. The sensation of being perched in an eyrie is heightened by a sudden riffle of feathers and rush of wings as a hawk stoops past, a dark missile travelling with terrifying velocity, to disappear into the trees after prey unknown. More sedately, a black woodpecker in search of insects spirals down a gaunt grey snag — a dead tree devoid of bark or branches. It would have been tidied away long since in a managed European forest. But this is not Europe. It is the west coast of British Columbia, a wild, ice–carved landscape, uninhabited but for a few logging camps and fish farms.

Round the corner of the cabin comes Skookum, the huge, good–natured Alsatian. He is being taunted by a squirrel that scolds and chatters from a safe distance up a tree. Cautiously, the squirrel inches its way down the fissured trunk, goading the dog to leap. Skookum is used to this game and waits motionless at the bottom. Finally, it is the squirrel's nerve that breaks and it shoots back up the tree with a squeal of annoyance.

The cabin is a simple affair of plywood sheets nailed to a wooden frame. To reduce damp and to prevent it being totally buried by snow in the winter, it has been built on four massive tree stumps, giving it the appearance of an old granary. A bucket has been placed upside–down over the chimney to keep out squirrels and pine–martens. Last winter another unwanted visitor, a grizzly bear, smashed open the door when the cabin was unoccupied and we are still finding polythene bottles punctured by teeth and claws in the bushes round about. Like it or not, one is very close to the natural world up here.

I am the guest of wilderness guides Rob and Laurie Wood, and the journey to their cabin has not been without effort. It started with the flight from Heathrow to Vancouver, the eight hour time change, backwards, enabling me to take a thirty minute onward flight to the little port of Campbell River on Vancouver Island the same day. Not as jet–lagged as anticipated, I caught the ferry across to Quadra Island the following morning. Rob and Laurie were waiting to drive me across the island to Heriot Bay, a small anchorage where their catamaran Quintano was moored. On the jetty we were joined by Tom and Julia, proprietors of the Heriot Bay Inn, who were taking a well–earned holiday after a long summer season.

There was not a breath of wind so Rob fired up the outboard and we motored through a maze of narrow tidal channels between islands and eventually up a long forested fjord to a deserted logging camp at its far end. The sun shone and we lazed about on deck, cans of beer in our hands. That night we ate dinner on the boat, and then Rob anchored her off–shore, returning in a canoe. Half an hour's walk up a bouldery river bed and an overgrown logging road, brought us to an empty cabin where we spread out our sleeping bags and fell asleep serenaded by croaking frogs.

The next day started easily enough, gradually gaining height on the old logging road, overgrown with alder trees through which a tenuous way is kept clear by the Woods and their friends. At lunch–time we lit a fire and brewed some tea to strengthen us for the spell of bush–whacking that lay ahead. For Rob, tea-making is an important ritual, slowing down the pace, drawing together the members of a group and encouraging them to be fully present in the moment.

Leaving the security of the old road, we forced our way through a tangle of alder branches and thickets of salmonberry, thimbleberry and the notoriously prickly Devil's Club. Fortunately, this was short–lived, and soon we emerged into first–growth timber, huge well–spaced trees spared by the chain saw. However, many of the trees had long ago been 'culturally modified' by the local Indians. Instead of felling trees, they would peel off long strips of bark, especially from cedars, to use as roofing material and even for clothing. The amount taken was not enough to damage the tree and the bark eventually grew again, but the long tapering scar remains as a reminder of a more sustainable silviculture than is usually practised today.

The hillside was steep now, and the going strenuous. Frequently we were skirting round or clambering over moss–grown fallen tree trunks or heaving ourselves up on the stems of blueberry bushes. With packs full of sleeping–bags, spare clothes and food for three nights, it was hot work and tiring. We were all glad when the trees began to thin out, the angle eased, and we finally reached the cabin.

Over mugs of tea and hunks of cake we discussed the problem of access. Rob and Laurie believe deeply in the need to retain or renew our links with the natural world and in the therapeutic and spiritual value of wilderness. At the same time they realize that the rugged nature and sheer scale of the British Columbian landscape can make it inaccessible to many people. The long walk from the sea, while part of the adventure for the young and fit, would be too much for many people. The option does exist to be flown up to the cabin by helicopter, enabling guests to enjoy the wonderful alpine world above in a manner as relaxed or as energetic as they choose. Rob is ambivalent about this, however, not wishing to deter the elderly or the disabled, yet wary of packaging wilderness or bowing to the convenience ethic.

For us, the next two days were by turn highly energetic and utterly relaxing. There was no hurry, no schedule and plenty of time to do whatever we wanted. When we were not hiking or bouldering on granite bluffs or helping with the chores, we would each wander off and find a quiet niche somewhere to read, or write or simply be alone. Despite the attractions of a hot bath and proper bed, it was with regret that we barred the cabin door securely against marauding grizzlies and headed down through the trees back to the sea.

# FLOWER RIDGE

A frog croaks briefly
dragonflies hunt dark water
the pool quietens

Bats swoop jaggedly
far peaks harden in amber
the pool is silent

Trees tall black outlines
teeming constellated sky
the pool disappears

Day's end journey's end
another step on the way
tired eyes close sleep comes

1994

# UMFOLOZI TRAIL (1996)

"If a white rhino comes for you, just step behind a tree and keep still. Usually it will veer off or simply charge past and keep on going. But if a *black* rhino charges, it's more serious. You must climb a tree — quickly!"

We look around at the prickly thorn trees in our immediate vicinity, none of which look either easy or inviting to climb, even in an emergency, and laugh in disbelief. But Mike, our lean, bearded leader, is not joking. He has been treed a number of times, once dangling by his arms with his feet only inches from the horn of an angry rhino.

He is briefing a group of eight at the start of a five-day Trail organized by the Wilderness Leadership School of Natal. Apart from my wife, Netti, and myself, they are all white South Africans. We have driven in a minibus three hours northwards from Durban to the Umfolozi game reserve. This is an area of 95,000 hectares famous for a conservation success story, the saving of the white rhino from extinction in the nineteen-sixties. Now, the bus has been parked out of sight of the dirt road, our rucksacks are packed and we are ready to set off into that section of the Park designated a Wilderness Area, where there are no roads and access is allowed only on foot.

"Where exactly are we going?" asks Stuart who lives not far away at Richards Bay on the coast, and has some knowledge of the area. "What's our route?" He served as an officer in the South African army for six years so he is used to reading maps and keeping tabs on his position out in the Bush. He is nonplussed when Mike replies: "I haven't decided yet. It really doesn't matter — where we are going is where we are …" There is silence while we digest this nugget of Zen wisdom. Mike has no map, it transpires — it is all in his head.

"How far are we walking today?" asks Natasha, a young secretary from Cape Town. "Far enough," Mike answers cryptically, "but not too far …," and he hoists his pack onto his back before he can be asked any more questions. Clearly he has no intention of being pinned down about destinations, not physical ones anyway.

The packs feel heavy at first but the straps and waistbelt can be adjusted to take the weight on hips as well as shoulders. Inside each pack is a sleeping bag, food for four nights, a full waterbottle and one piece of communal equipment such as a canvas water bucket, a large cooking pot, a folding metal tripod for cooking on or a light tarpaulin to rig between two trees as shelter should it rain. On top of all that we add our own spare clothing, torch, camera, sandals and washing kit. On the outside we each carry a small groundsheet and a sleeping mat of closed-cell foam, rolled up together tightly.

However, Mike proves to be right. We always travel "far enough" with these burdens, but it never seems "too far". Wilderness Leadership School Trails are not Outward Bound courses. The back-packs are simply a means of enabling us to live closer to nature than we ever do normally. We carry them only far enough to be beyond sight or sound of human habitation and to move camp every day to a new location.

"Oh yes, there's one more thing," Mike says casually. "Please give me your watches. You won't need them in the Bush and they will be much safer here." Startled, but compliant, we hand them over and Mike locks them inside the bus. We are, it seems, entering a realm where times, distances and schedules have no place. I sense that this could be a venture into the interior in more ways than one.

We set off in single file, Mike in front, Quagasa our Zulu game guard, veteran of many a skirmish with poachers and with scars to prove it, bringing up the rear. Both carry rifles. At first we walk through typical African savannah, or bushveld, flat-topped acacias dotted about scrubby grassland. Soon, however, the trees become denser, the shade darker, and we are picking our way with care through forest that feels somehow threatening. Later, Mike tells us that this spot is known as Ambush Alley from the close encounters that have occurred here with rhino, buffalo and lion. However we disturb only a huge bird that flaps away silently through the trees. "Spotted Eagle Owl" Mike whispers.

We emerge onto more open ground and make our way down to the banks of the Black Umfolozi river. We wade across as the sun goes down and make camp a hundred metres upslope from the river in a clearing among some thorn trees. Shortly afterwards, a white rhino and her calf come down to drink. We wonder whether we will have to pack up and move in a hurry, but they do not cross the river and we watch entranced until they disappear back into the bush.

Making camp is simple enough. We unroll our mats wherever we intend to sleep. One party fetches water from the river in the canvas buckets. Another collects firewood, keeping a wary eye open for scorpions or spiders on or under anything they pick up. Mike prepares the fireplace with care. Minimum impact camping is practised here and there must be no trace of our passing when we leave next morning. Instead of a circle of stones or digging a pit, he brings a pot full of sand and makes a raised circular mound on which the fire will be built. In the morning, the sand and the ashes will be mixed together thoroughly, like sand and cement, and then scattered over a wide area with the trowel.

The other use of the trowel is to dig a hole at least four inches deep when we go to the toilet and to fill it in afterwards, so that our faeces can quickly be broken down by bacteria in the soil. Toilet paper, which does not biodegrade easily and can be dug up by animals, is burnt on the spot with a lighter or wrapped in more paper and burned on the campfire. The fire itself is kept small and wood used sparingly even though there is no shortage, an example of practical conservation.

Once, a small, yellow scorpion scuttles down the piece of wood I have just placed on the fire. I make a mental note to be more careful in future. Scorpion stings are not life-threatening for adults but they are intensely painful for at least two days. Instead of killing the scorpion, Mike carefully catches it in a mug and releases it a hundred yards away. Nobody says anything. We have come together as a group too recently for ethical discussions just yet, but the message is not lost on us. Mike, we are discovering, is a man of few words, not given to delivering homilies. But actions speak louder than words, and his restraint in the use of resources and his evident respect for all living things have made an impression already.

Over the next four days we gradually become attuned to our surroundings. The four elements — earth, air, fire and water — assume an importance they would have had for our ancestors, though it has been lost in our everyday lives, and something deep in our psyches stirs in response. We sit and sleep on the ground. We become conscious of the direction and strength of the wind and the implications this has for our safety, carrying our scent to wild animals. We swim in the icy water of the Black Umfolozi (for this is June, the South African winter) and wash with biodegradable soap, specially provided. We gaze at a night sky alive with shooting stars, and learn new constellations — the Southern Cross, Scorpio ... The fire that we cook on and sit around for warmth and companionship in the evenings, is kept burning all night as a deterrent to animals. Every night we take it in turns to keep watch for an hour at a time. For that hour, each individual is responsible for the well-being of the rest of the group, and alert to every sound outside the small circle of firelight — be it the grunt of a leopard, the eerie howl of a hyena, or the sudden, startling crack of a twig nearby. But it is a time for reflection, also, and the hour never seems long enough ...

We see and discover much about the African Bush. We watch white and black rhino, and buffalo, cautiously, from downwind, acutely conscious of their size and power. We see giraffe, zebra, wildebeest, impala, nyala, warthog, hyena, baboon and crocodile, and learn to recognize the spoor and the droppings of some of them. We identify Bateleur and Crowned eagles and distinguish Cape vultures from Lappet-faced. We watch fascinated as a dung beetle resolutely pushes a monstrous ball of dung many times its own size. We carefully skirt around the elaborate webs of huge but beautiful Golden Orb spiders. One night we exchange calls, hoot for hoot, with a wood owl and his mate until eventually he perches overhead as we lie in our sleeping bags.

From Mike and old Quagasa we learn, too, of the importance of trees in traditional Zulu culture. There is the Marula, for instance, from the fruit of which beer and a spirit are made, while a nutritious oil is extracted from the kernel. The tree is a symbol of fertility and a bride will still carry a bough with her at her wedding. There is the Nthomboti, a very hard wood which burns well with a pungent smell, but which can cause sickness if used to smoke or roast meat. There is the Coward thorn, with its wickedly long, straight thorn which grows steadily thicker and longer with age. In the days of Chaka, the notorious Zulu king of the last century, one test of a warrior's stoicism was to stand unflinching as one of these thorns was driven through a fold of skin from his stomach. Should he fail this, or any other test, he was thrown from a cliff top ten metres or so onto the canopy of a massive old tree with thorns several inches long and hard as bone. Or there is the Wait-a-bit thorn, with a curved thorn pointing in one direction and a straight one in the other. It is sometimes called the Spirit tree, for if a Zulu dies and is buried away from home, his spirit must still be brought back by his relatives in the form of a branch from the tree; in fact, on a bus or train an extra ticket is bought to be occupied by the spirit-branch.

Slowly, we come to feel a part of the Bush ourselves. On the afternoon of the fourth day I wander away from camp, with permission, along a dried-up river bed. A buck of some sort crashes away through the undergrowth making me jump, then all is quiet. I sit beneath a large tree long enough for a vulture to return to its gigantic nest in the topmost branches. A pied crow flies in and conducts a raucous conversation with a friend some hundreds of metres away. When eventually I leave, I do so stealthily and avoid disturbing them. Climbing out of the riverbed on a well-used game trail, I come to a clearing with a solitary tree-stump, about a metre high, in the middle of it. This is a rhino scratching post, polished smooth by the rough hide of generations of animals. However, it is unoccupied at present and it is the perfect height to rest my backside against. Gradually the Bush comes back to life around me, until there are birds everywhere — iridescent green and purple sunbirds, scarlet-headed finches, emerald starlings, and many more. I feel accepted and at home. Three days ago I would have felt uneasy and uncomfortable here on my own. I would have been worrying about the presence of dangerous animals — rhino, buffalo, lion, snakes, scorpions ... Now I acknowledge that all these creatures could be nearby but feel that so long as I remain alert and regard them with respect, I will come to no harm.

I lean against that post for maybe an hour, senses tuned to every thing around me, before I become aware that for all that time I have been totally in the present. Not for a moment have I contemplated the past or made plans, however trivial, for the future. I have been totally in the here and now — calm, quiet, still, yet alert and utterly alive. I recall T S Eliot's words about "living, and partly living" and realize that on this Wilderness Trail I have been truly living.

That evening we walk as a group up the hillside behind camp to watch the sun set. Afterwards, around the fire, while Mike prepares stir-fried vegetables and rice, we talk about what the Trail has meant to us individually. For Stuart it has provided a perspective from which to review his everyday life — its frantic pace, the constant pressure to meet deadlines, the lack of time to spend with his family. For Dieter, a German-born businessman settled in the Cape, it has been nothing new. It is his fifth trail with the WLS. But he sees it as a vital re-connection with the natural world, a periodic reminder of the other side of life to 'getting and spending'. Netti describes her nerve ends as tingling, raw even, from the impact of so many new sensations. She finds it hard to put her feelings into words so, instead, quotes from R S Thomas's poem 'The Moor'

> It was like a church to me.
> I entered it on soft foot,
> Breath held like a cap in the hand.

Although neither of us are church-goers, I know exactly what she means and, recalling my vigil at the rhino-post that afternoon, the second stanza of the poem seems equally apt:

There were no prayers said. But stillness
of the heart's passions — that was praise
Enough; and the mind's cession
of it's Kingdom.

Later, I realize that our 'wilderness experience' has not occurred by chance.
The whole Trail has been orchestrated to make it possible for each one of us, in
different ways, to be 'touched' by the wilderness, for that is the raison d'être of
the Wilderness Leadership School.

The School is a small but remarkable organization that, over the last thirty
years, has taken 40,000 people out on Trail. It was founded by Dr. Ian Player,
then a conservation officer with the Natal Parks Board and largely responsible
for the saving of the white rhino, with help and encouragement from Sir Laurens
van der Post. The aim of the School was, and still is, to provide people in general,
but especially leaders and opinion-makers within society, with a profound, first-
hand experience of the African wilderness. This causes them not only to value
wild places and fight for their preservation, but also to see themselves as an
integral part of Nature with all the implications that can have on their everyday
lives and behaviour. From its inception in Umfolozi, the WLS has grown so
that it now has five branches in different parts of South Africa , five full-time
field officers, a sizeable administrative back up and a large team of dedicated
volunteers. Dr. Player maintains close links with WLS but today is more actively
involved with the Wilderness Foundation, an international body which promotes
the concept of wilderness worldwide and has helped to stage five World
Wilderness Congresses over the last twenty years. He is also a Trustee of the
Wilderness Trust, a UK charity inspired by the work of the WLS to do something
similar with young people, in particular, in the wilder parts of Britain.

At the end of our Trail, when our watches have been returned and the
members of our group have gone their different ways, Netti and I are privileged
to spend two days with Dr. Player at a nearby game lodge. We hear from his
own lips the story of the WLS and the extent to which his vision has been
shaped by the work of C G Jung. One of Jung's books was entitled, significantly,
*Modern Man in Search of a Soul*. It was Jung's belief, echoed by Ian Player and
by Laurens van der Post, that the crisis of our world has two root causes: one is
the divorce of our physical lives from the natural world, so that we no longer
feel ourselves a part of it; the other is the over-development of our rational,

analytical consciousness at the expense of the instinctive, intuitive side of ourselves that is expressed in dreams, myth, fantasy and art. We have become cut off from both inner and outer Nature. Traditional faiths have lost their authority and a loss of meaning in the lives of many people is reflected in the statistics for depression, suicide and mental illness. Wholeness can only be regained by acknowledging the 'primitive' side of ourselves and one of the most powerful and effective ways of doing so, Dr. Player believes, is through a wilderness experience. That experience is essentially a spiritual one. It has to be, if people are to change. Having a good time or learning more about wildlife is just not enough. It is a message that is endorsed again and again with passionate conviction during our stay in South Africa by everyone connected with the WLS. As Thoreau said long ago:

'In wilderness is the salvation of the world.'